Leaving Welfare

Leaving Welfare

Employment and Well-Being of Families that Left Welfare in the Post-Entitlement Era

Gregory Acs
Pamela Loprest

2004

W.E. Upjohn Institute for Employment Research
Kalamazoo, Michigan

Library of Congress Cataloging-in-Publication Data

Acs, Gregory.
  Leaving welfare : employment and well-being of families that left welfare in the post-entitlement era / Gregory Acs, Pamela Loprest
      p. cm.
    ISBN 0-88099-310-3 (pbk. : alk. paper)—ISBN 0-88099-311-1 (hardcover : alk. paper)
      1. Welfare recipients—United States.   2. Welfare recipients—Employment—United States.   3. Temporary Assistance for Needy Families Program)   4. Public welfare administration—United States.   I. Loprest, Pamela.   II. Title.
    HV95.A5965   2004
    362.5′568′0973—dc22
                              2004009577

W.E. Upjohn Institute for Employment Research
300 S. Westnedge Avenue
Kalamazoo, Michigan 49007–4686

The facts presented in this study and the observations and viewpoints expressed are the sole responsibility of the authors. They do not necessarily represent positions of the W.E. Upjohn Institute for Employment Research.

Cover design by Alcorn Publication Design.
Index prepared by Nancy Humphreys
Printed in the United States of America.
Printed on recycled paper.

**To
Sarah and Andrew and
Joseph, Anna, and Michael**

Contents

Figures

Tables

Acknowledgments

We would like to thank the many people and organizations that supported us and helped us complete this book. The W.E. Upjohn Institute for Employment Research provided core funding this project, and The Urban Institute shared a portion of the total cost. It would have been impossible to pull together the material for this book had we not received support from the Office of the Assistant Secretary for Planning and Evaluation of the U.S. Department of Health and Human Services (ASPE) to produce an earlier synthesis of findings from location-based studies of welfare leavers.

The book has benefited greatly from the thoughtful comments of Kevin Hollenbeck at the Upjohn Institute. Also, our initial thinking about comparing leaver studies was influenced and enhanced by the project officers for the earlier ASPE synthesis, Julia Isaacs and Matthew Lyon.

Our work in assessing the status of families leaving welfare builds on the work of many other researchers and state program administrators that conducted the leaver studies reviewed in this volume. They are too numerous to name, but we thank them all. Many of these studies would not have been conducted had it not been for the federal support provided by ASPE. In addition, ASPE's involvement in these studies contributed mightily to their quality and comparability. To this end, we must also thank ASPE's technical assistance contractor, ORC Macro, and especially the diligent work of Tammy Ouellette.

We are grateful to Tracy Roberts for her help culling through these studies, tabulating data, and preparing tables and graphics. We also thank Jennifer Holland, who picked up where Tracy left off. Finally, we would like to thank our colleagues and friends at The Urban Institute for their patience and support. And to our families, who have spent the better part of the past two years asking, "Is the book done yet?" We can finally say, "Yes!"

1
Introduction

The Personal Responsibility and Work Opportunity Reconciliation Act of 1996 (PRWORA) made sweeping changes to the U.S. system of support for low-income families with children. The law eliminated the old welfare program, Aid to Families with Dependent Children (AFDC), and replaced it with the Temporary Assistance for Needy Families (TANF) program. The principal goals of the TANF program are to reduce long-term dependence on cash assistance and to encourage self-sufficiency through work. To this end, the program mandated work for most welfare recipients and limited the length of time benefits could be received.[1]

The years following welfare reform witnessed unprecedented declines in welfare caseloads across the country. Many supporters of the new law, including President Clinton, declared welfare reform a success. But a growing chorus of voices questioned whether leaving welfare was an end in itself and began looking for evidence of how those families that left welfare were faring. One result of this questioning was a proliferation of studies examining the situations of former recipient families—welfare leavers.

This book pulls together in one place much of the vast array of resulting information on how welfare leavers are faring. It provides comparisons of welfare-leaver outcomes across geographic areas and supplements these results with national-level outcomes where available. We then draw out some general conclusions for welfare reform and for future study.

BRIEF REVIEW OF WELFARE REFORM

PRWORA encompassed a number of broad changes in social assistance programs. The central change in the legislation, often referred to as welfare reform, is the replacement of AFDC with TANF.[2] The TANF program gives increased flexibility to states to design their cash assistance programs within the framework of federally mandated work re-

1

quirements.[3] States are required to have an increasing percentage of their caseload (for an increasing number of hours per week) in work or federally specified work activities.[4] States must impose sanctions on individuals who fail to meet work requirements. The law also limited to five years the amount of time an adult, over her lifetime, could receive federally funded TANF benefits. Unlike AFDC, TANF is not an entitlement for those meeting specific income criteria. States can decide the conditions for receipt of benefits.

Under TANF, states used the new flexibility to implement a number of different strategies to increase work among recipients.[5] Some states made it easier to combine work and welfare by allowing recipients to keep a greater amount of their earnings before losing benefits, often referred to as expanding earned income disregards. Many states mandated work activities as a condition of benefit receipt with minimal exemptions. Some states require work activities up front, as a part of the application process. States have a range of sanctions for failing to comply with work requirements, from a small reduction in benefits to loss of the total grant until compliance. Although all states must abide by the federal five-year limit, some states impose shorter limits, as short as 15 consecutive months, while other states use state funds for long-term recipients, essentially eliminating the time limit for families.

As a result of the different choices made by states, welfare programs now vary broadly from state to state, ranging from very stringent to more lenient programs. Despite these differences, all states have made their programs more work-focused in response to the federal legislation (Nathan and Gais 1999).

WHY STUDY WELFARE LEAVERS?

The number of families on welfare (see Figure 1.1) has fallen by more than 50 percent since 1996, from about 4.5 million to just over 2 million in March 2003. In just the first two years after reform, more than a million families left the rolls. Although these families were no longer dependent on cash assistance, many questions remained about their circumstances. Had they moved into employment and attained self-sufficiency? Were families experiencing serious material hard-

Figure 1.1 Families Receiving AFDC/TANF

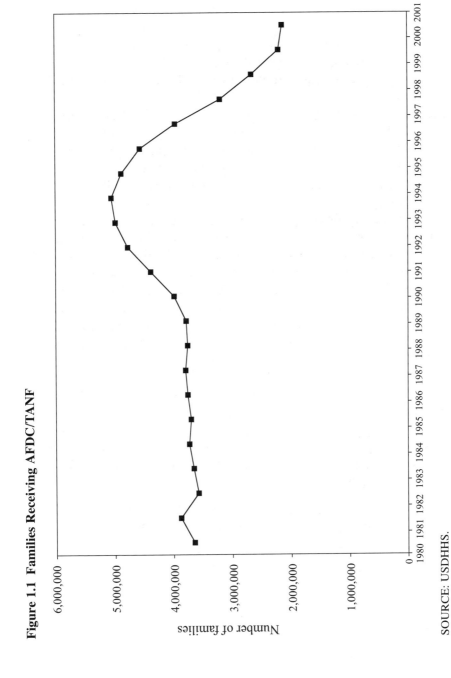

SOURCE: USDHHS.

ships? Did exit from welfare signal a long-term reduction in dependence?

The nature of the changes to welfare also prompted greater demands for information on how welfare leavers were faring. Before reform, it was generally assumed that anyone voluntarily leaving AFDC would do so because she was better off financially. Relatively few families were cut off welfare for non-economic reasons. Under TANF, more families can be cut from the rolls, because of either sanctions for not meeting requirements or time limits on benefits. Pressures of stricter new requirements, particularly work requirements, or the desire to "bank" future months of eligibility could also cause families to exit voluntarily.

After such major changes and steep caseload declines, there were many calls from the media, critics of the law, and welfare administrators for immediate information to understand the impact of welfare reform on families. While carefully designed evaluations are the only true way to measure the impact of welfare-reform provisions on families' behavior and outcomes, even in the best of circumstances, such studies could not produce answers for years to come. Studying the economic circumstances of leavers shortly after reforms, however, could provide valuable information relatively quickly.

Critics of the law, who had predicted serious unemployment and material hardship as a result of the changes, wanted to know whether these predictions had come true. Welfare program administrators, who were designing and implementing program changes, wanted to know the potential problem areas that needed to be addressed. Studies of leavers had the potential to shed light on a number of specific questions, including the following:

- Were families leaving welfare finding work? Was the observed caseload decline associated with increased employment?

- Were families that left welfare becoming self-sufficient, measured, for example, by income levels higher than poverty?

- What role were non-TANF government benefits playing in supporting leaver families?

- Were families that left welfare better off than when they were on welfare?

- Was there a subset of families that were experiencing significant hardship after leaving welfare? For example, was there any evidence for predictions of significant increases in homelessness, child abuse, or extreme poverty?

In response to the need for immediate information, government agencies and policy researchers conducted dozens of studies of welfare leavers in specific geographic areas. The best of these studies combine administrative data from states' welfare and Unemployment Insurance (UI) systems with surveys of TANF leavers. In addition, there have been several national studies of the status of welfare leavers using data from general-use surveys such as the National Survey of America's Families (NSAF) and the Survey of Income and Program Participation (SIPP), which can help place findings from location-based leaver studies in a national context.

WHY THIS BOOK?

This book provides the bottom line on what we know about the status of leaver families in the first years after welfare reform. Drawing on information from many of the location-specific leaver studies and other national-level research, we provide a comprehensive picture of the employment, income, and hardships families experience after leaving welfare. We also highlight problem areas for leaver families that could be addressed by future policy and program changes.

While other publications have summarized results from leaver studies,[6] this book goes beyond summary to draw out major findings, put them in the context of national results, and discuss what they mean for welfare reform.

For the many consumers of individual leaver studies, it is important to be able to put a single study's results in context. It is impossible to draw broad inferences from specific leaver studies because they cover only one geographic area. By examining results from multiple studies of different geographic areas, and in many cases comparing these to national results, we show whether a specific study finding is true more generally across the country.

It is also important to gain insight on the uniformity of national-level findings on the experience of families that left welfare. Our examination of results across geographic areas shows whether there is significant variation across the country on the economic situation of leaver families.

In addition, the outcomes of leavers vary considerably. Although we focus on the outcomes for the average leaver, much can be learned by examining the range of outcomes across different types of families, such as nonworking leavers and those who lost benefits due to sanctions. When possible, we highlight differences in how various subgroups of welfare leavers are faring.

Finally, welfare reform is an ongoing process. The 1996 changes were not the final word on "fixing" welfare, but one step, albeit a giant step, in a long line of changes that undoubtedly will continue into the future. For this reason, it is important to have a lasting record of what was learned after such a major policy change. This book endeavors to provide that record for one piece of the puzzle, understanding the status of families that left welfare.

CAVEATS TO USING LEAVER STUDIES

The conclusions one can draw from studying welfare leavers have limitations. Most studies of welfare leavers are not evaluations of welfare reform's impact on families leaving welfare. That is, they make no attempt to measure the extent to which welfare policy changes *caused* the outcomes (or changes in outcomes) that they report. They do not try to identify what would have happened to welfare leavers (or whether they would have left) in the absence of welfare reform. While many studies provide information on changes in measures for leavers before and after leaving welfare, this does not mean welfare reform caused any change. This fact needs to be kept in mind when drawing conclusions from these results.

By definition, leaver studies focus on families that not only have come in contact with the welfare system but who also have actually received benefits. Under welfare reform, formal diversion programs steer some applicants away from welfare, and some families, aware of the more stringent rules governing welfare, may not even bother to apply for benefits. The well-being of low-income families that stay off welfare is an important concern to those interested in the effects of welfare reform, but it cannot be addressed through leaver studies.[7]

In addition, comparing and synthesizing results from studies of welfare leavers must be done carefully, because there are many differences across them in both methods and site-specific factors. First, the quality and methods of individual leaver studies vary substantially. We draw here only from studies that used documented reliable methods, providing assurance that results are accurate. Second, the geographic areas in which the studies were conducted vary substantially in ways that could affect outcomes for welfare leavers. These differences include local labor markets, state and local welfare policies (such as generosity of benefits, sanctions, and time limits), other state policies (such as the availability of a state earned income tax credit or public health insurance), and the average characteristics of welfare caseloads.[8] All of these differences likely affect leavers' post-welfare experiences. We make no attempt here to ascribe specific variations in outcomes across studies to specific differences in study methods or sites. However, when discussing results, we highlight differences across studies where appropriate.

WHAT HAVE WE LEARNED?

The book is divided into four sections: methods used in welfare leaver studies (Chapter 2), work among leavers (Chapters 3 and 4), leavers who aren't working (Chapter 5), and the well-being of leaver families (Chapter 6).

Chapter 2 discusses the studies we focus on in this book, including how they were selected and the methods used in conducting welfare leaver studies.

Getting recipients to work was a major goal of the welfare reform legislation. Chapter 3 shows that the majority of welfare leavers across the country (about 60 percent) went to work. Although working leavers are paid, on average, comfortably more than the minimum wage, they do not have a comprehensive set of benefits. Indeed, fewer than half of all working leavers have paid sick leave, which means that any illness can cost them a day's pay and potentially their jobs.

Chapter 4 discusses issues of employment over time: job retention and earnings growth among leavers. During the first year after leaving welfare, overall employment rates for leavers remain fairly stable at around 60 percent. This overall stability, however, masks a certain amount of churning: on average, more than 7 in 10 leavers work at some point during their first year after exit, but only 4 in 10 work consistently. The average earnings of employed leavers in the fourth quarter after exit are 10 percent higher than the earnings of employed leavers in the first quarter after exit. Finally, while child care subsidies, food stamps, and Medicaid can improve the material well-being of working leavers—and therefore help them stay at work and off welfare—participation in these programs is quite modest.

Although many leavers left for work, many others did not. Chapter 5 discusses groups of leavers that have had a less successful experience under welfare reform. A substantial number of leavers are not working because they don't want or need to; that is, they prefer to care for their families at home or have a working spouse. However, many leavers are not working because they are in poor health or cannot find work. Some nonworking leavers return to welfare relatively quickly, indicating their initial exit did not lead to long-term independence from assistance. About one-fifth of all leavers in a given cohort return to TANF over the course of a year. Another 10 to 12 percent of families that left welfare have no earnings, have not returned to welfare, and have not transitioned to a public disability program. These families face multiple barriers to work and serious economic hardship. In addition, many who left welfare "involuntarily"—through sanctions for failure to follow rules—also have serious barriers to work and material hardships.

On average, leaver families have relatively low incomes and face significant material hardships. Chapter 6 reviews the evidence on family income and poverty as well as additional measures of leaver families' experiences with problems with food, housing, and health care. Despite some variation across geographic areas, most leaver families have, on average, relatively low incomes of $1,000 to $1,500 a month. About 40 to 50 percent of leaver families live in poverty, which is less than estimates of poverty among current welfare recipients. Measures of leavers' experience of food- and housing-related material hardships, while varied, show that about a quarter of leaver families experience at least some food- or housing-related problems after leaving TANF.

However, the evidence is mixed on whether these problems increase or decrease after exiting TANF, with some states finding an increase and some a decrease. The one exception is that more leavers have trouble accessing medical care after leaving TANF than when they were on TANF.

The results in Chapter 6 also emphasize the importance of work for the well-being of leaver families. Earnings are the primary source of income for leaver families, accounting for as much as three-quarters of family income. Families without a worker, not surprisingly, have substantially lower incomes. They also generally face greater material hardships.

All the findings from the leaver studies reviewed in this volume reflect the status of welfare leavers in the mid 1990s through the early years of the new millennium. During this time, the U.S. economy boomed and unemployment dropped to a 30-year low. Consequently, it is not unreasonable to expect that, during leaner economic times, leavers would face greater challenges moving from welfare to work and maintaining healthy families. Thus, to a certain extent, the findings synthesized here may represent a best-case scenario for welfare leavers.

Nevertheless, the information presented in studies of welfare leavers holds important implications for welfare policy and future re-search. For policy, it is clear that the majority of families leaving wel-fare are working, and the problems they face are similar to those faced by the working poor: relatively low pay, meager benefits, limited po-tential for growth, and unstable jobs. As such, programs that put more resources in the hands of working poor families can be extremely valu-able for improving the well-being of working welfare leavers. One ex-ample is expansion of the Earned Income Tax Credit (EITC), which provides a supplement to earnings for low-wage workers through the tax system, regardless of whether or not they owe taxes.

Because working leavers tend to have low wages and, at least at first, short job tenures, many are not eligible to collect UI should they lose their jobs. Consequently, their only recourse may be returning to TANF. States should consider using some of their TANF block grants to underwrite the cost of providing UI benefits to working leavers who are between jobs, which could reduce return rates to TANF and help leavers maintain their attachments to the labor market.

Instability of work, returns to welfare, and low to modest wage gains over time may also be a reflection of the poor quality of jobs for which many welfare recipients qualify. However, a focus on immediate work experience does not have to be mutually exclusive with education and training to "move up the ladder." Evidence shows that the most successful programs have a balance between immediate work and longer term skill-building activities (Gueron and Hamilton 2002), yet PRWORA limited the ability of states to count education and training activities as work activities, thus providing a disincentive for states to use these strategies. Changes in the law to remove these restrictions could encourage more long-term success in improving family incomes.

The well-being of working leavers could also be improved if they more fully participated in programs for which they are eligible, particularly child care subsidies, Food Stamps, and Medicaid. For example, many go without food stamps simply because it is hard to meet the administrative eligibility requirements, such as appearing in person to prove continued eligibility (recertifying) for benefits, while working. Expanding the hours of food stamp offices and/or allowing families to apply/recertify for benefits by mail, phone, fax, or Internet could help more working leavers make ends meet. A number of states are already implementing some of these changes.

In the same way, participation in Medicaid could be increased if enrollment were automatically extended to all leavers for three months without the need to redetermine eligibility. This would give state agencies time to contact leavers and provide them with information about transitional assistance. Other strategies to ensure leavers know they are eligible for benefits and to simplify procedures also need to be considered.

These policies could improve the material well-being of leavers and help them remain off the welfare rolls. In addition, these policies may have the added benefit of encouraging more families to leave welfare for work and shortening the length of time families spend on welfare.

FUTURE RESEARCH

Our work here also offers insights for how to make the most of future research on leavers. One of the impressive outcomes of the leaver studies is their contribution to increasing capacity of many state welfare agencies for undertaking research studies. The U.S. Department of Health and Human Services (USDHHS) has played a key role in this development through its provision of technical guidance and funding of a number of leaver, diversion, and other welfare-recipient studies. In addition, the desire to have information on how leavers are faring has prompted many states to undertake leaver studies even without federal funding. It is important to continue to build on these efforts.

One possibility for continuing research is for states to put out periodic tracking studies, using administrative data sources, of how new cohorts of leavers are faring. Many states that have conducted leaver studies have the capacity to link TANF program information with state UI data. If states were to link these two data systems as a matter of course, they would be able to monitor the work status of welfare leavers, track individual leavers' earnings growth over time, and monitor leavers receipt of benefits such as food stamps and Medicaid. The federal government could even require data-reporting elements of states.

In addition, broader efforts to continue research on how leavers are faring could be undertaken. While much basic information can be garnered from linked administrative data, survey data can provide a much fuller picture of the status of welfare leavers. Syntheses of individual place-based surveys of welfare leavers, such as this volume, are useful, but because of issues of cross-site comparability, they provide at best a patchwork understanding of how welfare leavers are doing. Similarly, national studies using current data are limited because general-use data sets do not have a sufficiently large number of families leaving welfare at the same time to allow for comprehensive analyses. Consequently, it would be useful to have a national survey of welfare leavers with samples drawn from state administrative data. Detailed uniform data on a national sample of leavers—especially if those data are longitudinal, capturing leavers at, for example, 6, 18, and 36 months after exit—would be an important resource for research. Such data would provide a comprehensive picture of welfare leavers across the nation and would allow researchers to examine how local policies, practices, and circumstances affect the status of these families.

Finally, it is also important to draw attention to the families that are not leaving welfare. Welfare "stayers" are likely to become a growing issue as more families start exhausting their lifetime TANF allotments. Understanding the needs and obstacles facing long-term stayers and helping them make and sustain transitions off welfare is an important area for future research. Indeed, the USDHHS has recognized this need and has funded six location-based stayer studies. Other states, using newly gained research capacity, could also carry out some study of current recipients using the USDHHS-developed survey instrument or a shorter variant. While conducting a survey is more expensive than using administrative data, it may be well worth the investment for state welfare agencies moving into the next stage of implementing welfare reform.

Since the passage of PRWORA, welfare caseloads have fallen dramatically. Studies of welfare leavers have helped us understand how families have coped with the transition off welfare. Many work; some cannot. Most are no worse off than they were while on welfare, while some have prospered and some have foundered. In the chapters that follow, we document what these studies have shown about the ability of leavers to find and retain jobs and the challenges they face. We conclude by discussing the implications these leaver studies hold for state and federal policy as well as identifying future research needs.

Notes

1. For a detailed review of the provisions of the 1996 law, see Greenberg and Savner (1996). For a brief overview of the law, see Chapter 1 in Blank and Haskins (2001).
2. In addition, the law included a reorganization and increase in funding for child care programs, limitations on Supplemental Security Income eligibility for children with disabilities, elimination of most noncitizens' eligibility for public assistance, and tougher food stamp and child support enforcement program rules.
3. Before PRWORA a growing number of states had received waivers to redesign their AFDC programs, many using the policies described here. Some of the state waiver experiences served as a model for the eventual federal law.
4. A provision to allow "credit" toward the work requirement for states' past caseload declines made meeting these requirements, at least for single-parent families, relatively easy for most states.
5. Other policy changes unrelated to work were also implemented, such as not increasing benefits for children born to mothers on TANF (known as a family cap) and requirements on paternity establishment.
6. Many of these studies have been reviewed in Acs and Loprest (2001a, 2002), Brauner and Loprest (1999), USDHHS (2000), and U.S. General Accounting Office (1999).

7. Several studies have used methods similar to those used in location-based welfare leaver studies to look at families that have applied for welfare but have been either denied or diverted (see http://aspe.hhs.gov/hsp/leavers99/rpts-apps.htm).

8. See Chapter 2 for a more detailed discussion of the differences in methods and other site-specific factors across leaver studies.

2
Methods Used in
Welfare Leaver Studies

The dramatic decline in welfare rolls during the mid 1990s spurred concern about how families that left welfare were faring. In response to these concerns, many states and substate areas began tracking families that exited welfare. Some of these early efforts used questionable methods such as mail surveys; others relied on very small sample sizes (e.g., fewer than 100 survey respondents) or achieved response rates that fell well below 50 percent.

A second generation of leaver studies built on the lessons learned from earlier efforts. One major factor in improving the quality of leaver studies was the federal government, under the auspices of the U.S. Department of Health and Human Services Office of the Assistant Secretary for Planning and Evaluation (ASPE). ASPE began to support these research efforts by funding a series of location-based leaver studies. The guidance and technical assistance provided by ASPE ensured that these studies followed sound methodological procedures and produced a group of leaver studies that used comparable methods, measures, and time periods. In this volume, we focus on 15 of these second-generation location-based leaver studies.

These 15 studies represent some of the best research on welfare leavers and include information from all regions of the country, from large and small states, and from major metropolitan areas (Table 2.1). This is not an exhaustive list of all high-quality leaver studies, and new studies continue to be produced. However, this set of studies does capture information from a wide set of jurisdictions, providing a cross-country picture of the early implementation of federal welfare reform.[1]

The location-based leaver studies we include all follow the same basic analytic approach:

- They focus on cohorts of leavers, defined as all families that stopped receiving welfare during a particular quarter. In most cases, a family has to remain off welfare for two consecutive months to be considered a leaver.

15

Table 2.1 Location-Based Leaver Studies Reviewed in this Volume

State	Author	Type of study	Leaver cohorts
Arizona	Westra and Routley 2000	Survey and administrative	1Q98
District of Columbia	Acs and Loprest 2001b	Survey and administrative	Two Cohorts: 4Q97, 4Q98
Florida	Crew et al. 2000	Survey and administrative	2Q97
Georgia	Bross 2001	Administrative	Three Cohorts: 1Q97, 1Q98, 1Q99
Georgia	Foster and Rickman 2001	Survey	Jan. 1999–June 2000
Illinois	Julnes et al. 2000	Survey and administrative	Six cohorts: 3Q97, 4Q97, 1Q98, 2Q98, 3Q98, 4Q98; Survey: Dec. 1998
Iowa	Kauff et al. 2001	Survey and administrative	2Q99
Massachusetts	MA Department of Transitional Assistance 2000	Survey and administrative	Dec. 1998–Mar. 1999
Missouri	Ryan 2001	Administrative	4Q96
Missouri	Midwest Research Institute 2001	Survey	4Q96
New York	Rockefeller Institute of Government and NY State Department of Labor 1999	Administrative	1Q97
South Carolina	Richardson et al 2001	Survey and administrative	Oct. 1998–Mar. 1999
Washington	Ahn et al. 2000	Administrative	Three cohorts: 4Q96, 4Q97, 4Q98
Washington	Du et al. 2000	Survey	October 1998
Wisconsin	Wisconsin Department of Workforce Development 2001	Administrative	2Q98–4Q98
Cuyahoga Co.	Verma et al. 2001	Survey and administrative	Two Cohorts: 3Q96 and 3Q98
Los Angeles Co.[a]	Verma and Goldman 2000	Administrative	3Q96
Bay Area	Mancuso et al. 2001	Survey and administrative	Two Cohorts: 4Q96, 4Q98

NOTE: See Table A.1 for more complete information on these leaver studies.

[a] Results in this volume for Los Angeles County are based on preliminary analyses available to the authors at the time these studies were collected.

- For each cohort of leavers, the studies use administrative records to examine leavers' subsequent use of cash assistance under TANF and their participation in the Food Stamp and Medicaid programs. Some studies have broader administrative data on leavers' participation in additional social support programs, such as child care subsidies and child support, as well as data from state child welfare agencies.

- Almost all studies link their administrative program data with data on employment and earnings from the state's UI system.

- The studies supplement their administrative data using surveys of TANF leavers. Generally, the survey samples are drawn from a single cohort of leavers. These surveys provide richer information about families than can be garnered from administrative data.

In addition, all 15 of the included studies fully describe the methods they used to identify leavers and assess their well-being, including information on such items as survey response rates. One additional advantage of the ASPE-funded leaver studies is that their data are publicly available. Using these data files, we were in several instances able to create more comparable measures, such as quarterly reports from monthly administrative data, and conduct further analysis, such as examining the share of total income by source and studying nonworking leavers not receiving TANF (see Chapters 5 and 6).[2] We only include results from surveys that achieved response rates of 50 percent or higher. Table 2.2 presents response rates, sample sizes, and other information for the studies examined in this volume.[3] The appendix provides additional information about the methodological issues involved in comparing and synthesizing leaver studies.

Because these location-based leaver studies all begin with state administrative records, they can capture all families that stopped receiving welfare in a particular location at a particular time. They are not plagued by the same reporting error found in general-use surveys. Indeed, general-use surveys must rely on self-reports of current or past welfare receipt to identify welfare leavers, and welfare receipt is traditionally underreported in surveys. Nevertheless, nationally representative general-use surveys such as the NSAF, the SIPP, and the Panel

Table 2.2. Survey Information

Study	Cohort date	Mode	Sample size	Response rate (%)	Timing of survey after exit
Arizona	1Q98	Phone, in person	821	72	12–18 months
District of Columbia	4Q98	Phone, in person	277	61	12 months
Georgia	Jan. 1999–June 2000	Phone, in person	—	—	8–12 months
Illinois	Dec. 1998	Phone, in person	514	51	6–8 months
Iowa	2Q99	Phone	401	76	8–12 months
Massachusetts	Dec. 1998–March 1999	Phone, in person	930	75	~10 months
Missouri	4Q96	Phone, in person	878	75	26–34 months
South Carolina	Oct. 1998–March 1999	Phone, in person	1,072	74	12 months
Washington	Oct. 1998	Phone, in person	987	72	6–8 months
Bay Area	4Q98	Phone, in person	438	66	6–12 months

NOTE: Georgia does not report information on sample size or response rate for the full cohort. — = not available.

Study of Income Dynamics have all been used to study welfare leavers at the national level. Throughout this volume we draw on results from research using these data to supplement findings from location-based leaver studies.[4]

Below, we examine some of the key methodological issues that must be addressed in conducting location-based leaver studies.

DEFINING THE STUDY POPULATION

The first issue all leaver studies must address is, "Who is a leaver?" It is clear that a leaver is someone who has stopped receiving welfare, but precisely how to define a leaver can vary.

It is not uncommon for a welfare case to be closed for administrative reasons—for example, the adult in the unit failed to appear for a recertification meeting. Sometimes cases closed for this reason reopen within a matter of weeks. These leavers were neither trying to exit welfare nor were they "forced off" by a formal sanction. To avoid including these administrative closures, studies often require that a case remain closed for two months before inclusion in the sample of leavers. Nevertheless, some studies require that a case remain closed for only one month. Although one might expect that, other things being equal, studies using a one-month definition would have higher returns to welfare, prior research indicates that is not the case (Acs and Loprest 2002).

In some cases, the adult(s) in a welfare case leave or are removed from an assistance unit, but their children continue to receive benefits. Some studies consider that adult to be a welfare leaver while others consider the case to remain open. Since the children still receive support and the mother may be in the household, just not in the assistance unit, classifying the mother as a welfare leaver may influence findings in multiple ways. For example, these "mother-only" leavers may be both less likely to return to welfare and less likely to work than a mother whose entire family leaves welfare.

Once a study adopts a definition of a leaver, it can choose to focus on all cases that fit the definition or exclude specific subpopulations from the analysis. The most commonly excluded groups are child-only cases, two-parent families, and leavers who return to welfare within a specified time frame. Even though a growing proportion of welfare cases are child-only cases, leaver studies are generally interested in adult-level outcomes such as employment. Consequently, most leaver studies exclude child-only cases.

Because most welfare cases with an adult present are single-parent cases, some studies focus exclusively on single-parent cases. Because two-parent leavers may have more "human" resources available to them—for example, one parent can provide "free" child care while the other works—excluding two-parent leavers may overstate the hardships faced by families leaving welfare. The importance of this choice depends upon the size of a location's two-parent caseload. Providing information for all leavers and for one- and two-parent cases separately is preferred, particularly in locations where there is a high proportion of two-parent cases.

Another important consideration in defining the study population is whether or not to restrict the sample to those families that remain off welfare for a specified amount of time. We refer to such leavers as continuous leavers. Although this term distinguishes between true leavers and families cycling on and off welfare, restricting an analysis to continuous leavers is a bit extreme. Returns to welfare are an important potential outcome for welfare leavers, and those who return to welfare most likely have lower rates of employment and higher participation in other programs such as Food Stamps and Medicaid. Nevertheless, it is useful to consider continuous leavers as a special subset of all leavers in any given study. For example, an examination of all leavers might find that the share receiving food stamps remains constant over time. But this approach might mask two countervailing trends: as time goes by, one group of leavers returns to welfare, thereby increasing food stamp participation, while another group of leavers, continuous leavers, has declining food stamp participation.

Another important subgroup to consider is families that were terminated from welfare by a sanction. Because sanctioned leavers may behave differently or have different characteristics than nonsanctioned leavers, separation of these results can be important, especially in areas where a significant portion of a given leaver group left due to sanctions. Results for all leavers in such an area could mask negative results for the subset of sanctioned leavers.

DATA USED IN LEAVER STUDIES

Studies of welfare leavers rely heavily on two types of data: state administrative records and direct surveys of welfare leavers. Each source can provide valuable but limited information about the well-being of welfare leavers.

Administrative Data

States have data systems used for administering programs, such as TANF, and these databases can be used in conducting leaver studies. Typically, state welfare program data can provide information on the timing of receipt of welfare benefits, the value of the grant, the number of people (adults and children) in the case, and some demographic characteristics of recipients, usually race, age, number and ages of children, and whether a case is single parent or two parent. Of course, availability of TANF data is critical to conducting a leaver study because it allows one to define who is a leaver. In addition, this information can be used to determine who among a group of leavers returns to welfare and some basic characteristics for conducting subgroup analysis. One can also examine records on participation prior to the month of exit to assemble a history of receipt. This information can be used to analyze subgroups based on being a long-term or short-term recipient, although none of the studies we review has carried out such an analysis.

State program data may include information on participation in the Food Stamp and Medicaid programs linked to TANF program data. Other types of program data may be available to be linked to TANF data. Only three of the studies listed here have made use of additional program data. Some examples of the types of data they examine include child care subsidies, receipt of child support payments, and involvement in the child welfare system. Information from such programs provides a richer description of the well-being of leavers.

By their nature, program data do not contain information on families that no longer receive program benefits. Consequently, there is no way to determine if leavers who do not return to the caseload and are not participating in other programs are finding jobs. To address this problem, many leaver studies use additional administrative data, linking their welfare program records to data from state UI systems. If a leaver is working for an employer that reports wages to the state UI system, then these linked records reveal whether a leaver is working in a given quarter and how much that leaver earned. Because the employment and earnings of welfare leavers are key outcomes for policymakers and researchers, linking administrative data from the welfare system with data from the state UI system is vital.

Note that using administrative data to assess the status of welfare leavers often requires researchers to link information across various data systems. In general, researchers use Social Security numbers to link information on welfare leavers with information from other sources such as UI earnings records. If there is a discrepancy in an individual's Social Security number across data systems, then no match can be made. Goerge and Lee (2002) provide a detailed discussion of techniques that can be used to improve the quality of matched data between administrative data systems.

Overall, the greatest strength of administrative data is that they provide accurate information on program participation for all leavers who continue to reside in the state. Information on employment and earnings from UI records is also reliable; however, leavers who work outside of the state or in jobs that do not generate UI wage reports[5] will not be in a state's UI system.[6] Thus, administrative data on employment probably understate employment among leavers. The greatest weakness of administrative data is their failure to provide information on many aspects of well-being and changes in family structure. Thus, they provide a limited picture of the status of TANF leavers.[7]

Survey Data

Surveys of welfare leavers are particularly good at obtaining information that is beyond the scope of administrative data systems. For example, in addition to employment and wage information, a survey can obtain data on job characteristics — nonwage benefits, training, and work-related expenses. Surveys also can elicit information on changes in a leaver's personal characteristics and household composition as well as what sort of hardships the leavers have faced. Further, leavers can be surveyed even if they have moved across state lines.

Surveys of welfare leavers generally collect information on a sample of families that left TANF during a specific time frame by interviewing them some number of months after their exit. There are advantages and disadvantages to the choice of how long after exit to interview respondents. The shorter the time between exit from welfare and the interview, the more able a former welfare recipient is to recall information on the circumstances around leaving, such as reason for leaving and specifics of their first job. The longer the time between exit and interview, the more information about a family's transition can be gathered.

Most studies gather survey information using telephone interviews, but many also conduct some in-person interviews. This combination method ensures that leavers without telephones are included in the study. Overall, the strength of survey data is the breadth of information they contain. However, survey data have their own set of shortcomings. First, surveys rely on respondents to answer questions accurately and truthfully.[8] Second, survey data are collected for only a sample of welfare leavers; as such, any assessment of the well-being of leavers based on surveys is subject to sampling error. Finally, and perhaps most seriously, even if the sample of leavers accurately reflects all leavers, not all sampled families will respond to the survey. That is, a researcher will only be able to contact and interview a subset of the original sample. If the leavers who respond to the survey are very different from the nonrespondents, then the survey data will suffer from nonresponse bias and will not accurately represent the status of leavers. The best way to reduce nonresponse bias is to have a high response rate. There is a large literature on increasing response rates (see Cantor and Cunningham 2002; Singer and Kulka 2002; Weiss and Bailar 2002).

Leaver studies can employ two relatively straightforward techniques to assess the extent of nonresponse bias in surveys of welfare leavers. The first technique involves using administrative data on the entire survey sample and comparing respondents with nonrespondents. The second involves using the survey data to compare the characteristics of easily located and interviewed leavers with those of leavers that were hard to find.[9]

Acs and Loprest (2002) discuss several studies that use administrative data to compare respondents and nonrespondents. These studies differ in the measures used to compare respondents and nonrespondents. Dunton (1999) reports that in Missouri that nonrespondents tend to have less education and lower quarterly earnings than respondents. Edelhoch and Martin (1999) find that in South Carolina, respondents are significantly less likely to have their cases closed because of a sanction and significantly more likely to have their cases closed because of earned income than nonrespondents. The District of Columbia study reports that respondents are fairly similar to nonrespondents, although nonrespondents are slightly younger, have younger children, and have had shorter spells of receipt than nonrespondents.

Another technique to gauge the importance and potential biases of nonresponse involves examining differences among respondents, comparing survey responses from respondents who were easy to contact and quickly agreed to be surveyed with the responses of hard to contact and reluctant responders.[10] This approach is based on the idea that hard-to-interview cases fall on a continuum between the easy to interview and nonrespondents. If the hard to interview are very different from the easy to interview in ways that are important to the study, it is likely that nonrespondents are even more different, and nonresponse bias is likely to be a big problem.

Using this technique, the District of Columbia study finds that hard-to-interview cases are neither clearly better off nor clearly worse off than the easy-to-interview cases; rather, their experiences are more diverse. For example, easy-to-interview cases are slightly more likely to work than hard-to-interview cases, but among those who work, the hard-to-interview have higher hourly wages. In a supplementary study, Dunton (1999) compares employment and earnings among survey respondents in the Kansas City area based on the timing of response. Dunton finds that respondents among the final third of completed interviews are slightly less likely to work than respondents in the first two-thirds of completed interviews. The harder-to-interview also have lower monthly incomes.

Although nonresponse analyses can be quite useful in gauging potential biases in surveys of welfare leavers, they do not help to establish a target response rate for such surveys. In an earlier review of the methods used in welfare leaver studies, Acs and Loprest (2002) examine the relationship between response rates and the reported employment rates of welfare leavers across a host of leaver studies. They find that employment rates across studies with response rates of more than 50 percent are fairly tightly grouped. Indeed, even though a response rate of 50 percent is moderately low, the average outcomes of welfare leavers can be captured. This probably occurs because of the heterogeneous nature of nonrespondents. That is, the leavers who are the least likely to be located and/or respond to surveys are those who are particularly successful and those who have lost everything. As such, leaver studies with moderate response rates provide fairly dependable information on the average outcomes of leavers; however, they do not reliably capture the outcomes of both leavers experiencing the most extreme hardships and those enjoying the greatest post-exit success.

SUMMARY

By combining administrative and survey data, the location-based leaver studies included in this volume provide valuable information on the status of families leaving welfare. Because they begin with state welfare caseload records, they reliably capture families leaving welfare. And by tracking families through both administrative welfare and wage records, the location-based leaver studies can provide information on work, returns to welfare, and use of other public support programs. Administrative data, however, have some important limitations. For example, families that leave the jurisdiction are lost to a state's administrative records, and not all jobs are recorded in state UI wage records. In addition, administrative data provide limited information on a family's overall well-being. Consequently, the best leaver studies, like the ones included in this volume, also conduct surveys of welfare leavers. These surveys enhance our understanding of the status of welfare leavers by collecting information on job-related benefits and measures of material hardship.

Notes

1. For a more limited review of the findings from earlier location-based welfare leaver studies, see Acs and Loprest (2002).
2. Restrictions apply to the use of these data. See http://aspe.hhs.gov/hsp/leavers99/datafiles/index.htm for details.

3. Unfortunately, although the included studies are all carefully done and are more or less comparable, it is not feasible to use information from the studies to perform a meta-analysis. Indeed, there are enough subtle differences between the included studies (e.g., how many months after exit the survey interviews are conducted) and omissions (e.g., most studies do not provide standard errors on their point estimates) to preclude a meta-analysis.

4. Other major multipart projects that are studying the impacts of welfare reform, including The Urban Change Project (housed at MDRC) and the Welfare, Children, and Families: A Three City Study (housed at Johns Hopkins University), have produced information on welfare leavers but have not conducted full-blown leaver studies as described here. These sources are cited where appropriate throughout the text.

5. Most jobs are reported to a state's UI system. Some exceptions include certain jobs in agriculture, self-employed workers, and household employees whose employers often fail to meet reporting requirements.

6. The Missouri study is the only one to examine UI data from a neighboring state (Kansas), and the District of Columbia is the only study to use employment and earnings data from the National Directory of New Hires.

7. For a thorough review of the limitations of using administrative data, see Hotz and Scholz (2002).

8. For a discussion of measurement in error in surveys of low-income populations, see Mathiowetz, Brown, and Bound (2002).

9. One can also attempt to do a retroactive study of nonrespondents. This is rather costly and involves painstaking efforts to locate nonrespondents to the initial survey and interview them. None of the studies reviewed here attempts this; however, Mathematica Policy Research is conducting such a nonrespondent study in Iowa. Their goal is to locate and interview 15 nonrespondents.

10. Groves and Wissoker (1999) use a similar approach for examining nonresponse bias in the NSAF.

3
Leaving Welfare for Work

A central goal of welfare reform is moving families from welfare to work and, ultimately, to self-sufficiency. In this chapter, we examine how successful families have been in making the initial transition from welfare to work. We begin by focusing on employment rates and earnings for leavers during the first quarter after exit; we also discuss the factors that helped them find their first jobs after exiting welfare. Finally, we discuss the characteristics of the jobs they hold.

HOW MUCH ARE WELFARE LEAVERS WORKING?

The majority of recipients leaving welfare go to work. Figure 3.1 shows that, on average, about three out of five leavers work in the first quarter after exit. Employment rates are remarkably consistent across leaver studies. The median first post-exit quarter employment rate across the studies is 57 percent, and many studies cluster tightly around the median. Indeed, in the first quarter after exit, employment rates range from a low of 47 percent in Los Angeles County to a high of 68 percent in Cuyahoga County.

These employment rates are all based on administrative data, generally from state UI systems.[1] These records include information on employment and earnings on all reported jobs a leaver has held during the quarter. While most working leavers' jobs and earnings will be captured in state UI data, jobs and pay from work in other states or in jobs not covered by the UI system (e.g., agriculture or self-employment) will be missed. Consequently, these employment rates likely represent a lower bound for the extent of work among welfare leavers. Indeed, when leavers are asked directly in surveys if they are working, the estimated employment rates are 2 to 7 percentage points higher than those reported in administrative data (Acs and Loprest 2001a). Further, an analysis of data from the 1996 SIPP shows that 64 percent of single mothers that exited welfare worked within four months of exiting (Acs et al. 2001). Similarly, an analysis of Panel Study of In-

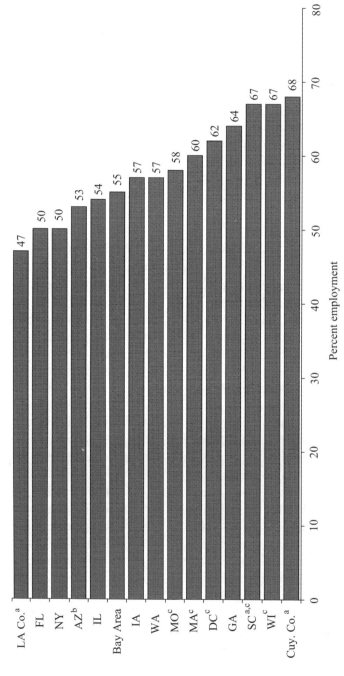

Figure 3.1 Employment in the First Quarter after Leaving Welfare

Percent employment

LA Co.[a] 47
FL 50
NY 50
AZ[b] 53
IL 54
Bay Area 55
IA 57
WA 57
MO[c] 58
MA[c] 60
DC[c] 62
GA 64
SC[a,c] 67
WI[c] 67
Cuy. Co.[a] 68

[a] Los Angeles Co., Cuyahoga Co., and South Carolina require a leaver to have at least $100 in earnings to be considered working, while others require only $1.

[b] Data from report differ from revised data provided by the state. Revised fourth quarter employment is 51% and ever worked after exit is 70%. Arizona added 17 new cases to the data file one year after the report was published.

[c] Report employment data for all cases, not just for single-parent cases.

SOURCE: Based on administrative data from leaver studies. See Table A.3 for a complete listing of the leaver studies cited.

come Dynamics data from the early 1990s shows that about two-thirds of all welfare exits are associated with work (Hofferth, Stanhope, and Harris 2001).

Employment rates for leavers are fairly consistent across locales despite the fact that leaver studies do not all use the same definition for employment. In most cases, a leaver is considered to be employed if she earned at least $1 during a calendar quarter. Several studies require leavers to show a stronger commitment to working before counting them as employed. For example, the South Carolina, Los Angeles County, and Cuyahoga County studies require a leaver to have at least $100 in earnings to be considered working. Interestingly, these differences do not account for much of the meager variation across studies. Although Los Angeles County did have the lowest employment rate, Cuyahoga County and South Carolina report the highest employment rates despite using this higher threshold for employment.

All these employment measures are fairly broad—even in the three studies using the $100 earnings threshold, a leaver would be considered employed if she earned federal minimum wage ($5.15 an hour) and worked for just one-half of 1 week out of a 13-week quarter. Our tabulations of data files from Arizona, the District of Columbia, Florida, Illinois, Iowa, and South Carolina allow us to examine employment rates using a stricter definition of employment: an earnings requirement of at least $500 in a quarter. This higher threshold basically requires a leaver to have worked roughly the equivalent of 5 part-time (20-hour) weeks and be paid minimum wage to be counted as having worked in a given quarter. Figure 3.2 shows that, under this tighter rule, employment rates in the first post-exit quarter are 6 to 11 percentage points lower than under the "any earnings/$100 earnings" criterion. Only about one-half of all leavers work and earn at least $500 in their first quarter after exit. Under this stricter definition of employment, employment rates for leavers range from a low of 42 percent in Florida to a high of 56 percent in the District of Columbia and South Carolina.

The noticeable difference in the employment rates obtained when using low and moderate earnings thresholds may indicate that a nontrivial portion of welfare leavers counted as working in these studies actually work very little in the first post-exit quarter. However, it is important to keep in mind that quarterly UI wage data generally reflect calendar quarters. Thus, the first post-exit quarter for a woman who

Figure 3.2 Employment in the First Quarter after Leaving Welfare Using a $500 Earnings Threshold

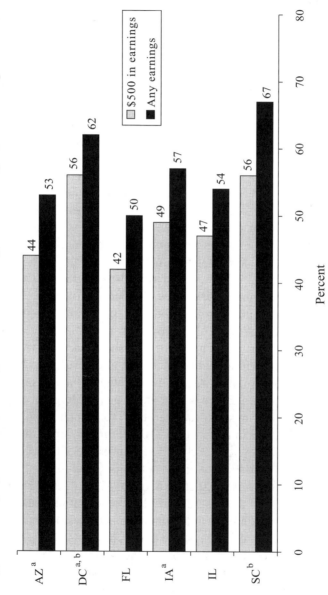

[a] Authors' calculations from leaver study data files.
[b] Report employment data for all cases, not just for single-parent cases.
SOURCE: Based on administrative data from leaver studies. See Table A.3 for a complete listing of the leaver studies referenced.

leaves welfare in January would run from April through June. This time frame means she could obtain a job in January, work throughout February and March, but lose her job in early April. Despite working for three months, her earnings in her first post-exit quarter (April through June) would be quite low, yet she still clearly worked. Another scenario under which the first post-exit quarter earnings are quite low could arise when a woman is sanctioned off welfare at the end of a calendar quarter (say, March) and takes several months to find work during her first post-exit quarter (which in this example runs from April through June). Even though she has worked very little during the quarter, the presence of any recorded earnings indicates she has found a job.

Thus, whether it is an artifact of the way these data are compiled or an indication that some leavers work only a trivial amount, very low earnings in the first post-exit quarter do show that a leaver worked. Any leaver who generates reported earnings in a quarter has, at the very least, shown that she can obtain a job; she has made contact with an employer and tried to work. As such, it is useful to distinguish between leavers who work even a small amount and those who do not work at all. That some leavers have very low earnings in their first post-exit quarters (and in later quarters, as we discuss in Chapter 4) serves to highlight the importance of examining more than just employment when assessing the status of welfare leavers.

HOW DID WORKING LEAVERS FIND THEIR JOBS?

While a substantial share of leavers work, there is a paucity of information on how they find jobs. The few studies that gather this information find that there is no single pathway to employment for working leavers, although interpersonal job networks are quite important. Indeed, more than one-third of working leavers in the District of Columbia used friends and relatives to find jobs, and about one-third of Florida's working leavers say that these informal networks are the most important vehicle for finding work. Directly contacting potential employers is a job search method used by a substantial portion of working leavers. Interestingly, public employment agencies and the welfare office are somewhat less important for leavers who found work—about one in five relied on these institutions to help find work.

HOW MUCH ARE LEAVERS PAID?

Although more than half of all leavers work in the first three months after exit, their earnings are quite modest. Figure 3.3 shows that the mean earnings of employed leavers during the first post-exit quarter range from about $1,900 to about $3,400.[2] Even at the high end of this scale in the District of Columbia, the quarterly earnings of the average working leaver hover around the poverty level. While there is substantial variation across studies, it is important to note that many studies cluster around the median, $2,663. Indeed, half the studies find mean earnings in the first post-exit quarter ranging from about $2,200 to $2,800 for leavers with any earnings.

Again, these earnings figures include the earnings of women who did very little work during their first quarter off welfare. Figure 3.4 shows earnings for leavers earning more than $500 a quarter and compares them with leavers with earnings of any amount. We find that among leavers who did more than just cursory work during their first quarter off welfare, average earnings are $300 to $400 higher than average earnings of all employed leavers. Using the stricter definition of employment, we see that average first-quarter earnings range from $2,609 to $3,757.

For the most part, UI wage records provide information on earnings. These records include earnings information on all reported jobs a leaver has held during the quarter. Earnings from employment not covered under UI are not included. Further, the data provide no information on the number of weeks or hours leavers actually worked to achieve their earnings.[3] To obtain a more detailed view of the jobs working leavers hold, we must turn to survey data.

WHAT KINDS OF JOBS DO WORKING LEAVERS HOLD?

The survey components of leaver studies generally obtain information on the job(s) leavers hold at the time of the survey rather than the

Figure 3.3 Mean Earnings in the First Quarter after Leaving Welfare

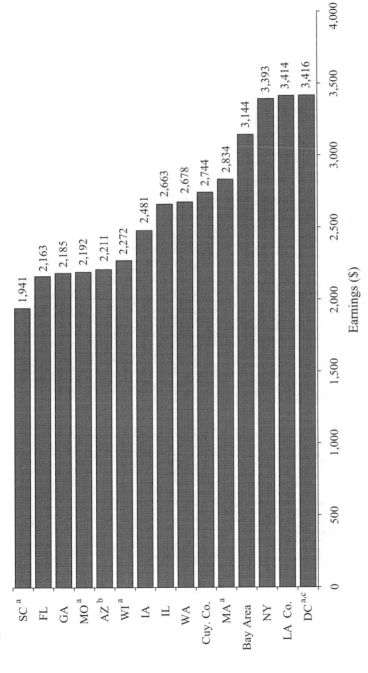

Earnings ($)

[a] Report earnings data for all cases, not just for single-parent cases.
[b] Data from report differ from revised data provided by the state. Revised fourth quarter earnings are $2,525. Arizona added 17 new cases to the data file one year after the report was published.
[c] Data reported for District of Columbia are median earnings, not mean earnings.
SOURCE: Based on administrative data from leaver studies. See Table A.3 for a complete listing of the leaver studies cited.

Figure 3.4 Mean Earnings in the First Quarter after Leaving Welfare

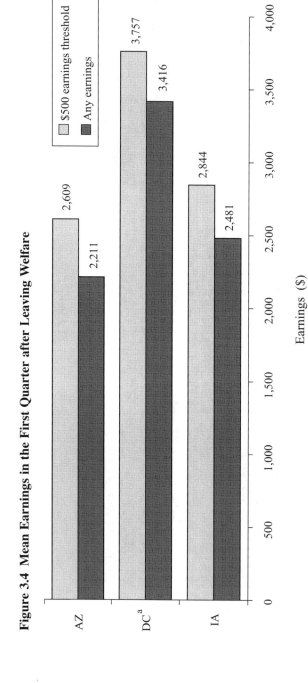

NOTE: Authors' calculations from leaver study data files.
[a] Report earnings data for all cases, not just for single-parent cases. Earnings data for DC are median earnings, not mean earnings.
SOURCE: Based on administrative data from leaver studies. See Table A.3 for a complete listing of the leaver studies cited.

job(s) they were working at when they exited welfare. Surveys in the studies reviewed here were conducted 6 to 18 months after exit. Consequently, the leavers who are working at the time of the survey may have experienced some wage growth since exit and may have become eligible for more employer-sponsored benefits.

Since information on jobs is based on reports from the leavers themselves, surveys capture employment in jobs that UI administrative data miss (e.g., jobs in another state and self-employment). In studies that report both administrative and survey-based employment rates, the rates based on survey data run 2 to 7 percentage points higher than rates based on administrative data (Acs and Loprest 2001a).

Survey findings indicate that employed leavers work close to full-time on average, with mean weekly hours ranging from 33 to 39 and median hours (when reported) reaching 40 (Table 3.1). Mean hourly wages range from $7.50 to $8.74, and median hourly wages range from $6.50 to $9.00. This median hourly wage is similar to the $7.15 rate Loprest (2001) finds using national data.

Although employed leavers are mainly working full-time hours, they are not necessarily employed consistently. If a leaver works 40

Table 3.1 Hours and Wages of Welfare Leavers

State/study	Hours worked		Wage rate ($)	
	Mean	Median	Mean	Median
Arizona	35	—	7.52[a]	—
District of Columbia[b]	36	40	8.74	8.13
Illinois	—	37	7.89	7.41
Iowa	35	—	7.54	—
Massachusetts[b]	33	—	8.46	—
Missouri	39	40	—	—
South Carolina[b]	—	—	—	6.50[c]
Washington	36	40	7.70	7.00
Cuyahoga County	35	—	7.50	—
Bay Area	—	—	—	9.00

NOTE: — = not available.
[a] Data published in the report differ slightly because they have been recalculated by authors using current sample weights.
[b] Report data for all cases, not just for single-parent cases.
[c] For those who have not returned to welfare.
SOURCE: Based on administrative data from leaver studies. See Table A.3 for a complete listing of the leaver studies cited.

hours a week and earns $7.50 an hour, she would earn $3,900 in a quarter provided that she worked all 13 weeks in the quarter. However, as illustrated above, quarterly earnings are usually less than $3,900, indicating that a substantial share of leavers experience periods of joblessness.

Although these average reported wage rates fall within what one would reasonably expect a lower-skilled worker without recent work experience to earn, it is important to consider the distribution of working leavers' wages. Table 3.2 shows the 25th, 50th, and 75th percentiles for hourly wage rates of leavers. Working leavers in the bottom quartile of earners have hourly wage rates that fall below $6 to $7. These rates illustrate two important points: a substantial minority of working leavers have very low wages and the majority of leavers earn substantially more than the federal minimum wage. Table 3.2 also shows that, in the higher cost of living areas of the District of Columbia and Massachusetts, the top quartile of working leavers earn more than $10 an hour. In Iowa and Arizona, the top quartile of leavers earn more than $8 an hour.

In addition to monetary pay, employed leavers may receive noncash employee benefits through their jobs. Table 3.3 shows that there is considerable variation in benefits coverage across locations. For example, the share offered employer-sponsored health insurance on their jobs ranges from 36 percent in Washington to 61 percent in Iowa. The

Table 3.2 Hours and Wages of Employed Welfare Leavers and Overall Employment Rates

	Hours worked		Wage rate ($)			
State/study	Mean	Median	Mean	25th percentile	Median	75th percentile
Arizona[a]	35	40	7.52	6.00	7.00	8.50
District of Columbia[a,b]	36	40	8.74	7.00	8.13	10.00
Iowa[a]	34	38	7.19	6.00	7.00	8.00
Massachusetts[a]	34	35	8.46	6.50	8.29	10.00
South Carolina[b]	36	—	—	—	—	—

NOTE: — = not available.
[a] Authors' calculations from leaver study data files.
[b] Report data for all cases, not just for single-parent cases.
SOURCE: Based on administrative data from leaver studies. See Table A.3 for a complete listing of the leaver studies cited.

Table 3.3 Percent of Employed Welfare Leavers with Employer-Sponsored Benefits

| | Benefit | | | | |
| | Health insurance | | | | |
State/study	Offered	Covered	Paid sick leave	Paid vacation	Pension
Arizona	—	12	—	—	—
District of Columbia[a]	—	32	50	62	46
Iowa	61	33	40	60	—
Massachusetts[a]	52	—	47	55	—
Missouri[a]	53	—	40	52	—
Washington	36	19	28	31	21
Cuyahoga County	58	27	50	63	—
Bay Area	41	—	—	—	—

NOTE: — = not available.
[a] Report data for all cases, not just for single-parent cases.
SOURCE: Based on administrative data from leaver studies. See Table A.3 for a complete listing of the leaver studies cited.

share of leavers actually covered under employer-sponsored health insurance plans is much lower, ranging from 12 percent in Arizona to 33 percent in Iowa. At the national level, NSAF data indicate that 23 percent of working leavers have employer-sponsored health insurance (Loprest 1999). Even those with access to health insurance through their employers may have to contribute toward premium costs and make copayments when they visit health care providers. Note that leavers without employer-sponsored health coverage may have public health insurance coverage through the Medicaid program or they may be covered under a working spouse's policy.

Other important benefits include paid sick leave, paid vacation, and pension plans. Table 3.3 shows that less than half of all working leavers have paid sick leave, which means that any illness can cost them a day's pay and potentially their jobs. The share of leavers with paid sick days ranges from a low of 28 percent in Washington to a high of 50 percent in the District of Columbia and Cuyahoga County, with Massachusetts close behind at 47 percent. In the other two studies reporting this information (Iowa and Missouri), about two out of five leavers have paid sick leave. Paid vacation days are more common than sick days among working leavers. In three studies, the share with paid vacations reaches 60 percent or more (District of Columbia, Iowa, and Cuyahoga County). Nevertheless, vacation days generally need to be requested in advance and provide only limited protection to workers to attend to personal or family emergencies. Finally, 46 percent of working leavers have retirement benefits in the District of Columbia, compared with 21 percent in Washington.

Variations in pay and benefits likely reflect differences in the employment mix across geographic areas. Unfortunately, many leaver studies do not report the industry and occupation of working leavers, and the ones that do report this information do not consistently report data on wage rates and benefits. Nevertheless, it is still useful to consider the types of jobs that leavers hold and note how they vary across studies.

Table 3.4 shows the distribution of working leavers across broad industry and occupation categories for both a national sample of leavers and for a set of leaver studies reporting this information (Richer, Savner, and Greenberg 2001). Overall, 46 percent of working leavers are employed in the service sector, while 24 and 14 percent are employed in retail trade and manufacturing, respectively. The remaining 16 percent work in other industries such as agriculture or transportation. Turning to occupation, national data indicate that 38 percent of leavers are in service occupations, 19 percent are in administrative occupations, 12 percent are in sales, and 31 percent are in other occupations.

Overall, a clear majority of families leaving welfare go to work. Although working leavers are paid, on average, above the minimum

Table 3.4 Industry and Occupation of Employed Welfare Leavers (%)

Industry	National	IA	SC	WI	
Service	46	44	57	48	
Retail	24	29	16	25	
Manufacturing	14	8	19	15	
Other	16	19	8	12	
Occupation	National	IL	IA	MO	SC
Service	38	39	37	53	37
Administrative	19	20	17	7	14
Sales	12	16	16	16	21
Other	31	25	30	24	28

SOURCE: Richer, Savner, and Greenberg (2001).

wage, they generally do not have a comprehensive set of benefits. Indeed, less than half of all working leavers have paid sick leave or pension benefits.

In many respects, working welfare leavers are similar to other low-income working mothers. Loprest (1999) uses NSAF data to compare working welfare leavers with working women living in families whose incomes fall below 150 percent of the federal poverty level and who have never received welfare. She finds that working leavers and other low-income working mothers generally work in the same industries and occupations. However, working leavers have higher hourly wage rates and are more likely to work full time than low-income mothers who did not receive welfare.

As working leavers spend more time on the job, they may enjoy both wage growth and expanding benefits coverage. However, it is important to note that job characteristics are measured several months after a working leaver exited welfare. As such, the wage rates and benefits already can reflect some growth in the job. In the next chapter, we examine the progress working leavers make during the first year following leaving welfare.

Notes

1. The District of Columbia's leaver study accessed data from the National Directory of New Hires (NDNH) to obtain quarterly employment information for its TANF leavers. This data source cuts across state lines and includes federal workers; thus, given the District of Columbia's geography and employment patterns, NDNH has more complete and more useful information for the District of Columbia than do state UI records.

2. Note that we report nominal monetary values. While inflation was very low during the late 1990s, a two-year difference between studies can represent about a 5 percent difference in purchasing power.

3. There is some concern that earnings in the first post-exit quarter are artificially low because UI wage reports reflect calendar quarters (see discussion earlier in text). However, using the second post-exit quarter to assess earnings is also problematic because some leavers who worked for three or more consecutive months after exit will lose their jobs during the second post-exit quarter. Acs and Loprest (2001a) show that average earnings in the second post-exit quarter are only slightly higher than earnings in the first post-exit quarter, and this may well be due to wage growth.

4
Staying at Work

The transition from welfare to work is not necessarily a smooth or permanent change. Women may return to welfare or cycle on and off welfare for some time. Some leavers will come to rely on family, friends, and perhaps other government transfer programs. Here we consider the employment patterns of welfare leavers to assess the extent to which they are able to work steadily and whether work effort and earnings increase over time.

EMPLOYMENT PATTERNS

The proportion of leavers working in any given quarter after exit remains fairly stable over the first post-exit year at about 60 percent (Table 4.1). If anything, a slightly smaller portion of leavers work in the fourth post-exit quarter than in the first post-exit quarter.[1]

Although overall employment rates for former TANF recipients are relatively constant, the same individuals who work in the first quarter do not necessarily continue to work throughout the year. Indeed, there is a considerable amount of instability in the employment patterns of individual welfare leavers. As Table 4.2 shows, the share of leavers who ever worked in the first year after exiting in the median study is 71 percent. In contrast, the share of workers with earnings in all of the first four post-exit quarters ranges from 35 to 39 percent in the median studies. Thus, leaver studies from across the country show that about 7 in 10 work at some point during the first year after exit; 4 out of 10 work consistently (reporting hours in each of their first four post-exit quarters), and 3 in 10 work sporadically.

These findings are based on very low earnings thresholds — a leaver is considered working if she earns as little as $1 in a given quarter. Table 4.3 shows employment rates and employment growth in selected sites using minimum earnings of $500 per quarter. Not surprisingly, employment rates are lower; however, the same basic story emerges. Employment rates change little between the first and fourth post-exit

41

**Table 4.1   Change in Employment of Welfare Leavers During First
Post-Exit Year**

| State/study | Welfare leavers employed post-exit (%) | | Change[a] |
	Q1	Q4	
Arizona	53	50[b]	-3
District of Columbia[c]	62	60	-2
Florida	50	54	4
Georgia	64	57	-7
Illinois	54	55	1
Iowa	57	38	-19
Missouri[c]	58	58	0
New York	50	48	-2
South Carolina[c,d]	67	63	-4
Washington	57	57	0
Wisconsin[c]	67	67	0
Cuyahoga County[d]	68	64	-4
Los Angeles County[d]	47	57	0

[a] Percentage point change.

[b] Data from report differ from revised data produced by the state. Revised 4th quarter
employment is 51% and ever worked after exit is 70%. Arizona added 17 new cases
to the data file one year after the report was published.

[c] Report employment data for all cases, not just for single-parent cases.

[d] Los Angeles County, Cuyahoga County, and South Carolina require a leaver to have
at least $100 in earnings to be considered working, while others require only $1.

SOURCE: Based on administrative data from lever studies. See Table A.3 for a complete listing of the leaver studies cited.

quarters. The share of leavers who work in any of the four post-exit
quarters ranges from 60 to 70 percent, and the share of leavers who
work in all four quarters hovers around 30 percent.

One possible explanation for the stability of overall employment
rates may be that many leavers who work in the first quarter after exit
lose or leave their first post-exit jobs and end up returning to welfare.
If we focus on leavers who managed to remain off welfare—continuous
leavers—we might expect to see more employment growth. Surprisingly, this scenario does not hold true. Table 4.4 shows that employment rates for continuous leavers are virtually identical in the first and
fourth post-exit quarters in most studies. Iowa even reports a sharp
drop in employment. Further, the share of continuous leavers who work

Table 4.2 Share of Welfare Leavers Ever Working Post-Exit and Working Consistently in First Post-Exit Year

State/study	Ever worked after exit (%)	Worked all four quarters (%)
Arizona	73[a]	—
District of Columbia[b]	79	39
Florida	71	31
Illinois	70	39
Iowa	69	25
Massachusetts[b]	68	—
New York	62	40
South Carolina[b,c]	90	34
Wisconsin[b]	82	—
Cuyahoga County[c]	82	47
Los Angeles County[c]	57	35

NOTE: — = not available.

[a] Data from report differ from revised data produced by the state. Revised 4th quarter employment is 51%, and ever worked after exit is 70%. Arizona added 17 new cases to the data file one year after the report was published.

[b] Report employment data for all cases, not just for single-parent cases.

[c] Los Angeles County, Cuyahoga County, and South Carolina require a leaver to have at least $100 in earnings to be considered working, while others require only $1.

SOURCE: Based on administrative data from leaver studies. See Table A.3 for a complete listing of the leaver studies cited.

Table 4.3 Employment Patterns of Welfare Leavers Using $500 per Quarter Earnings Threshold

State/study	Post-exit quarter (%)			Worked all four quarters (%)	Ever worked after exit (%)
	Q1	Q4	Change[a]		
Arizona[b]	44	44	0	25	62
District of Columbia[b,c]	56	54	-2	35	74
Florida	42	46	4	—	63
Illinois	47	48	1	—	63
Iowa[b]	49	32	-17	20	61
South Carolina[c]	56	53	-3	—	—

NOTE: — = not available.

[a] Percentage point change.

[b] Authors' calculations from leaver study data files.

[c] Report employment data for all cases, not just for single-parent cases.

SOURCE: Based on administrative data from leaver studies. See Table A.3 for a complete listing of the leaver studies cited.

**Table 4.4 Employment Patterns of Single-Parent Welfare Leavers—
Continuous Leavers**

State/study	Post-exit quarter (%)			Worked all four quarters (%)	Ever worked after exit (%)
	Q1	Q4	Change[a]		
Arizona	53	52	-1	36	68
District of Columbia[b,c]	63	64	1	44	80
Iowa	55	39	-16	28	67
Washington	57	56	-1	—	—

NOTES: — = not available. All data are calculated from public-use data files.
[a] Percentage point change.
[b] Report employment data for all cases, not just for single-parent cases.
[c] Corrected employment rates for continuous leavers in the District of Columbia; published rates are incorrect.
SOURCE: Based on administrative data from leaver studies. See Table A.3 for a complete listing of the leaver studies cited.

in any of the four post-exit quarters as well as the share working in all four quarters are quite similar to the rates reported for all leavers.

That the employment rates for continuous leavers are so similar to those for all leavers is consistent with the idea that continuous leavers are a particularly heterogeneous group. While some are stably employed and experience wage growth, others likely left welfare through changes in living arrangements or by transitioning on to other public assistance programs, such as Supplemental Security Income (SSI). Indeed, Loprest (1999) finds that 47 percent of nonworking leavers receive support through SSI, Social Security, and/or child support. Those who left welfare for nonwork reasons may be more likely to stay off the rolls than those who left welfare for work. As such, average employment rates for continuous leavers closely resemble the employment rates for all leavers.[2]

EARNINGS PATTERNS

Although employment rates for leavers do not grow during the first year after exit, the earnings of leavers do rise over time. Because leaver studies examine earnings growth using UI wage records, we cannot determine the extent to which growth in average earnings reflects higher hourly wage rates or growth in the amount of time spent at work from quarter to quarter.

Table 4.5 shows the change in the average earnings of leavers between their first and fourth post-exit quarters. On average, we see that quarterly earnings increase by about $300, or more than 10 percent, over the year. The studies report a fairly wide range of findings, from virtually no change in the Cuyahoga County study to almost a $600 increase in Washington State. Five studies report changes in earnings of less than 10 percent, while three report increases of more than 20 percent.

These earnings gains may be due in part to greater experience, increases in hours worked, the weeding out of less able workers, and improvements in the worker–job match over time. Research on wage

Table 4.5 Earnings Growth of Employed Welfare Leavers

State/study	Post-exit quarter ($) Q1	Q4	Change ($)	Change (%)
Arizona	2,211	2,511[a]	300	13.6
District of Columbia[b,c]	3,416	3,934	518	15.2
Florida	2,163	2,496	333	15.4
Georgia	2,185	2,327	142	6.5
Illinois	2,663	2,959	296	11.1
Iowa	2,481	2,712	231	9.3
Massachusetts[b]	2,834	—	—	—
Missouri[b]	2,192	2,698	506	23.1
New York	3,393	3,602	209	6.2
South Carolina[b]	1,941	2,332	391	30.1
Washington	2,678	3,275	597	22.3
Wisconsin[b]	2,272	2,561	289	12.7
Cuyahoga County	2,744	2,754	10	0.4
Los Angeles County	3,414	3,576	162	4.7
Bay Area	3,144	—	—	—

NOTE: — = not available.

[a] Data from report differ from revised data provided by the state. Revised 4th quarter earnings are $2,525. Arizona added 17 new cases to the data file one year after the report was published.

[b] Report earnings data for all cases, not just for single-parent cases.

[c] Data reported for District of Columbia are median earnings, not mean earnings.

SOURCE: Based on administrative data from leaver studies. See Table A.3 for a complete listing of the leaver studies cited.

growth among former welfare recipients suggests that earnings growth reflects increases in both hours worked and hourly wage rates. Johnson and Corcoran (2003) find that the median wage rates on the jobs held by former and current welfare recipients in Michigan grew by 15.9 percent over a two-year period. They also report that the share of employed women working full-time rose from 46 to 65 percent. The growth in full-time employment is quite important because wage growth is stronger for full-time workers. Loeb and Corcoran (2001) show that former welfare recipients who work full time enjoy real wage growth of about 6 percent per year. Note, however, that even with wage growth of 6 percent, a welfare leaver who takes a job paying $6 per hour would be earning about $7.50 per hour four years later.

It is important to note that the earnings growth figures reported in leaver studies are based on the difference between the average earnings of leavers employed in the first post-exit quarter and the average earnings of leavers employed in the fourth-post exit quarter—the same leavers do not necessarily make up both groups. To see how earnings change for the same set of workers, we must look at studies and data for leavers who work in each of their first four post-exit quarters.[3] One would expect that, because these leavers are consistently if not continuously employed, they would show greater than average earnings growth. Table 4.6 shows that, in three studies with this information, this growth does not occur. In the District of Columbia, the average earnings of consistent workers actually dropped; in Arizona and Iowa,

Table 4.6 Earnings Growth of Consistently Employed Welfare Leavers

State/study	Post-exit quarter ($)		Change ($)	Change (%)
	Q1	Q4		
Arizona[a]	2,645	2,938	293	11.1
District of Columbia[b,c]	5,007	4,836	-171	-3.4
		3,240	239	8.0

[a] Data from report differ from revised data provided by the state. Revised 4th quarter earnings are $2,525. Arizona added 17 new cases to the data file on year after the report was published.
[b] Report earnings data for all cases, not just for single-parent cases.
[c] Data reported for the District of Columbia are median earnings, not mean earnings.
SOURCE: Based on administrative data from leaver studies. See Table A.3 for a complete listing of the leaver studies cited.

average earnings grew by slightly less than earnings of all leavers in those two studies.

Although average earnings growth rates are not higher for consistently working leavers than for all leavers, their earnings levels are considerably higher. For example, leavers who will work in all four post-exit quarters earn $234, $1,591, and $338 more than the average working leaver in the first post-exit quarter in Arizona, the District of Columbia, and Iowa, respectively. Thus, it may be the case that leavers who work consistently either land better jobs straight off welfare or bring better skills to their first jobs than other working leavers. Leavers who work intermittently may enjoy bigger earnings gains for several reasons: they may move from jobs for which they are ill-suited to jobs which are better matches for them, they may receive big rewards as they build basic skills, or they may be increasing the number of hours and weeks they work over time.

Consistent workers are not necessarily continuous workers—they may experience periods of joblessness and even return to welfare for brief periods. Another way to identify the most committed welfare leavers is to restrict the analysis to families that remained off welfare for an entire year. Table 4.7 shows that in some studies these continuous leavers experience greater earnings growth between their first and fourth post-exit quarters than working leavers in general. While there is little difference in earnings patterns between all and continuous leavers in Arizona and the District of Columbia, continuous leavers' earnings grew by 16.0 percent in Iowa (compared with 9.3 percent for

Table 4.7 Earnings Growth of Welfare Leavers—Continuous Leavers

State/study	Post-exit quarter ($)		Change ($)	Change (%)
	Q1	Q4		
Arizona[a]	2,470	2,771	301	12.2
District of Columbia[a,b]	3,685	4,275	590	16.0
Iowa[a]	2,634	3,056	422	16.0
Washington	2,945	3,750	805	27.3

[a] Authors' calculations from leaver study data files.

[b] Report earnings data for all cases, not just for single-parent cases. Earnings data are median earnings, not mean earnings.

SOURCE: Based on administrative data from leaver studies. See Table A.3 for a complete listing of the leaver studies cited.

all leavers) and by 27.3 percent in Washington (compared with 22.3 percent for all leavers).

These figures suggest that, in general, those leavers who remain off of welfare earn more after exit and experience more rapid earnings growth than the average leaver. It is not clear if higher earnings enable continuous leavers to stay off welfare or whether it is continuous leavers' skill and perseverance that allow them to be more successful in the labor market.

Whether focusing on all leavers, consistently working leavers, or continuous leavers, all the approaches to examining earnings growth discussed above count leavers with very low earnings in a quarter as working. If a greater proportion of working leavers work for only a week or two in the first exit quarter relative to the fourth quarter, then earnings growth may be overstated. However, as Table 4.8 shows, when the analysis of earnings growth is restricted to leavers earning at least $500 in a quarter, we find growth comparable to that reported for all leavers.

SUPPORTS FOR WORKING LEAVERS

To remain at work, employed leavers must balance the needs of their families with the demands of their jobs. This struggle can be particularly challenging for welfare leavers, who are by and large sin-

Table 4.8 Earnings Growth of Welfare Leavers Using $500 per Quarter Earnings Threshold[a]

State/study	Exit cohort	Post-exit quarter earnings ($)		Change ($)	Change (%)
		Q1	Q4		
Arizona	1Q98	2,609	2,899	290	11.1
District of Columbia[b]	4Q97	3,757	4,217	460	12.2
Iowa	2Q99	2,844	3,184	340	12.0

[a] Authors' calculations from leaver study data files.
[b] Report earnings data for all cases, not just for single-parent cases. Earnings data are median earnings, not mean earnings.
SOURCE: Based on administrative data from leaver studies. See Table A.3 for a complete listing of the leaver studies cited.

gle parents with limited material resources. Indeed, if the costs of going to work are prohibitively high and are taking a toll on family life, lower-paid working leavers may find that going to work is simply not worth it and return to welfare if they are still eligible for benefits. Under TANF, however, the relative costs of work and welfare are changing. With sanctions, time limits, and work requirements playing prominent roles in state TANF programs, it may be harder for women to choose welfare over even the most difficult employment situations. Support from family, friends, and government benefits can help working leavers overcome the challenges and stay employed.

The most basic need for working leavers is access to child care—finding caregivers to watch their children and being able to pay for this service. Beyond child care, working leavers must have sufficient material resources to make ends meet while working in low-paying jobs. The Food Stamp Program can provide in-kind assistance to many low-income working leavers, which allows them to use their earnings for other family needs. Finally, like all families, welfare leavers need access to health care, but many do not have health insurance through their employers. For these working leavers, the Medicaid or State Children's Health Insurance Program can meet this need. In this section, we examine the extent to which working leavers are accessing these sources of support.

Child Care

Because the transition from welfare to work is a major goal of many states' welfare programs, the need for child care among TANF leavers is an important consideration. Child care subsidies are generally available to employed TANF leavers, depending on their income level. Receipt of these subsidies is contingent on the type of care arrangement leavers use, their knowledge about and eligibility for subsidies, and the ease with which subsidies can be accessed. Concerns about the quality of care given to children of working TANF leavers are also important, although measures of child care quality are generally beyond the scope of the surveys conducted.[4]

Table 4.9 shows results for four studies that report child care usage information for employed leavers.[5] Iowa and Washington report results for leavers with children under age 13 and find that about 80 percent

Table 4.9 Child Care Arrangements among Employed Welfare Leavers (%)

Type of care	IL[a,b]		MO		IA[b]	WA[a]
	<6 years old	6–12 years old	<6 years old	6–13 years old	<13 years old	<13 years old
Uses nonparental child care	93	90	75	40	78	82
Type of arrangement for those using child care						
Relatives/siblings	58	59	41	42	65	41
Center/after-school care/ church or club	12	8	26	36[c]	14	23
Family day care/babysitter in home	15	16	18	8	35	13
Friends/neighbors	9	12	13	11	6	—
Preschool/Head Start	2	NA	3	NA	4	NA
Other	5	5	—	—	1	24[d]

NOTE: — = not available; NA = not applicable.

[a] Study reports of type of arrangement are recalculated to reflect percentage of families using nonparental child care.

[b] State reports results for leavers in work, job search, education, or training. Illinois reports results for all leavers, not just single parents.

[c] Includes school-sponsored programs.

[d] "Other" includes multiple arrangements, preschool/Head Start, child self-care, employer-sponsored care, and unspecified care.

SOURCE: Based on administrative data from leaver studies. See Table A.3 for a complete listing of the leaver studies cited.

of working leavers use some form of nonparental care. Illinois reports findings separately for working leavers with young children (under age 6) and for school-age children (ages 6–12) and finds nonparent child care utilization rates of 90 percent or more for both groups. In contrast, Missouri reports that only 75 percent of working leavers with children under age 6 and only 40 percent of with school-age children use nonparent care.

The types of nonparental care used have a number of similarities.[6] Relatives and siblings are the most common source of care for preschool and school-age children. The rate of relative/sibling care reported for working leavers in these studies ranges from 41 percent for preschoolers in Missouri to 65 percent for all children in Iowa. The next two most common types of child care arrangements after relative/sibling care are center-based care (including after-school care, churches, and clubs mainly relevant for older children) and family day care/babysitter care in the home. Missouri and Washington find center care to be the second most common type of arrangement, while Illinois and Iowa find greater use of family day care/babysitters.

Paying for child care is a critical issue for families leaving TANF for employment. Costs of child care and child care subsidies can affect, and often determine, the choice of arrangements. Table 4.10 shows that the share of employed leavers with child care arrangements who reported paying for child care for at least one child ranges from two to three out of every five employed leavers in the studies that report this information. The Missouri study breaks out this information by age of the child and finds that 38 percent of employed leavers with a child under age 6 pay for child care compared with 46 percent for those with school-age children.

Another issue of cost of child care for working leavers is their use of government child care subsidies. In the average study, about 20 percent of families use this type of assistance. Given that many families do not have a nonparental child care arrangement, and generally less than half of families that have an arrangement pay their providers for care, it is not surprising that relatively small percentages of leaver families report using child care subsidies. This suggests that families do not need them. However, we cannot rule out the possibilities that leavers do not know they could obtain these subsidies, that these subsidies are unavailable to them, or that the subsidies are difficult to use.

Table 4.10 Welfare Leavers Paying for Child Care

State/study	Percent of leavers with child care arrangements who are paying for care	Percent of leavers using subsidies	Average monthly costs for families making payments ($)
District of Columbia[a]	—	5 welfare 3 (private sources)	—
Illoinois[a,b]	44	17	211
Iowa[b]	55	17	244
Massachusetts[a]	61	43	165
Missouri[a]	40	14[c]	277
Children <6 years old	38	—	221
Children 6–13 years old	46	—	171
South Carolina[a,d]	61	26	—

NOTE: — = not available.
[a] Results are for all cases, not just single parents.
[b] Percentage includes those working as well as those in job search, education, or training.
[c] 36% have used subsidies at some point since exit.
[d] Results are for families that remain off of welfare at the time of the survey.
SOURCE: Based on administrative data from leaver studies. See Table A.3 for a complete listing of the leaver studies cited.

Research suggests that it can be quite daunting to access and use child care subsidies. For example, Adams, Snyder, and Sandfort (2002) note that, in some states, welfare leavers not only have to apply for subsidies in person but also have to return to the office to report changes in their employment situations and recertify for child care subsidies. Such practices are not universal, but they do create obstacles for leavers seeking child care assistance. Similarly, state practices on payments and paperwork requirements also affect the willingness of child care providers to accept children using subsidies (Adams and Snyder 2003).

Finally, consider the average monthly costs for child care among families paying for care. The average monthly cost ranges from $165 in Massachusetts to $277 in Missouri. Missouri also reports on cost by age of child, showing that costs for young children (under age 6) are lower than for older children (ages 6 to 13), $221 compared to $171. National data from the 1999 NSAF indicate that poor working families spend $227 per month (roughly 18 percent of their earned income) on child care (Giannarelli, Adelman, and Schmidt 2003).

Food Stamps

Because families with incomes up to 130 percent of the poverty level are eligible for food stamps, many working leavers are eligible for the program; by subsidizing the cost of food, food stamps effectively increase family income and well-being. We examine food stamp receipt among working leavers using survey data; thus, both are measured at the time of the survey, several months to a year after the woman exited welfare.

Figure 4.1 shows that only about one-third of working leavers receive food stamps. Food stamp participation rates for working leavers range from 26 percent in the District of Columbia to 49 percent in South Carolina. Even though food stamps could provide a substantial supplement to a leaver's income, many leavers do not take up benefits. Failure to take up food stamp benefits may occur because leavers do not realize they are eligible for benefits. It is also important to remember that for at least some working leavers, their incomes may be too high for them to be eligible for benefits.

These findings from leaver studies are consistent with work on food stamp take-up rates among low-income working families (Zedlewski 2001). Nevertheless, it is a general concern as to why welfare leavers and needy families fail to take up benefits for which they are eligible. Research suggests that while some low-income working families would receive such a small allocation of food stamps that it is not worth the trouble, other families that want the benefits have trouble meeting the administrative requirements. For example, a single mother who works during regular business hours may not be able to take time off from work to recertify her eligibility for food stamps with the program office. Recognizing these administrative hurdles, all 50 states have simplified their income-reporting requirements (U.S. Department of Agriculture 2003).

Medicaid

Leavers with incomes of up to 200 percent of the poverty level can receive health insurance under the Medicaid program, usually for about one year after leaving welfare for work. Although one-quarter to one-third of working leavers have health insurance through their jobs, em-

Figure 4.1 Share of Employed Welfare Leavers Receiving Food Stamps at the Time of Survey[a]

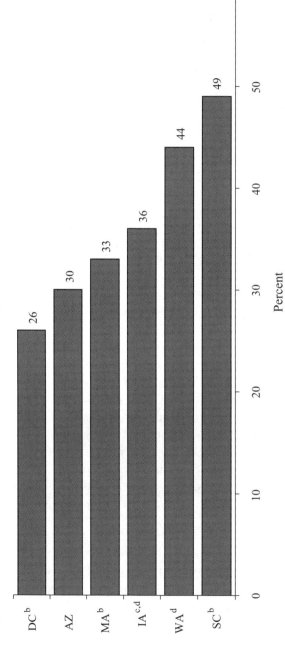

[a] All figures except South Carolina based on authors' calculations from leaver study data files.
[b] Results are for all cases, not just single-parent cases.
[c] Month prior to survey.
[d] Figures are for time since exit from welfare.
SOURCE: Based on administrative data from leaver studies. See Table A.3 for a complete listing of the leaver studies cited.

ployer-sponsored health insurance is not the norm. For many leavers, continuing Medicaid benefits can be an important work support.[7]

Figure 4.2 shows that the proportion of working leavers enrolled in Medicaid varies widely across locations. For example, in Massachusetts and South Carolina, more than four out of every five working leavers are enrolled in Medicaid. In contrast, the share enrolled in Medicaid is two out of five or less in Arizona, the District of Columbia, and Iowa.

Many working leavers are uninsured even though coverage may be available to them. For example, if a woman leaves welfare upon finding a job and loses contact with the welfare office, the state will terminate her welfare benefits; she and her children will be dropped from the Medicaid rolls as well. Such leavers may be unaware that they could continue to receive Medicaid.

The well-being of many working welfare leavers could be improved if they participated in the Food Stamp and Medicaid programs and received child care assistance. Indeed, some women who ended up returning to welfare may have been able to stay off had they been able to take advantage of these programs. Loprest (2002b) shows that only 19.2 percent of leavers who received government health insurance returned to welfare compared with 27.3 percent of leavers without government coverage. Similarly, leavers receiving help paying for child care are far less likely to return to welfare than those receiving no child care assistance (14.7 versus 24.7 percent).

SUMMARY

During the first year after leaving welfare, overall employment rates for leavers remain fairly stable at around 60 percent. This overall stability, however, masks a certain amount of churning: on average, more than 7 in 10 leavers work at some point during their first year after exit, but only 4 in 10 work consistently. The average earnings of employed leavers in the fourth quarter after exit are, on average, 10 percent higher than the earnings of employed leavers in the first exit quarter. Interestingly, however, this growth is not predicated on staying employed. Consistently employed leavers start out with higher earnings but do not experience more earnings growth than leavers who

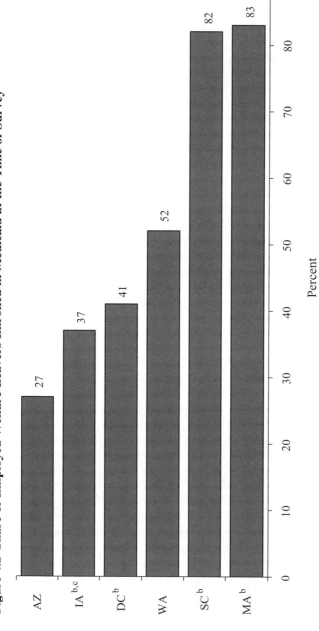

Figure 4.2 Share of Employed Welfare Leavers Enrolled in Medicaid at the Time of Survey[a]

Percent

[a] All figures except South Carolina based on authors' calculations from leaver study data files.
[b] Results are for all cases, not just single-parent cases.
[c] Month prior to survey.
SOURCE: Based on administrative data from leaver studies. See Table A.3 for a complete listing of the leaver studies cited.

were jobless for at least one quarter during the first year after exiting welfare. These data suggest that leavers who experience some prolonged joblessness after exiting welfare may ultimately be moving to better jobs or at least to jobs that are a better fit for them. Nevertheless, it is important to note that the average leaver in the average study earns well below $3,000 in the fourth post-exit quarter.

Adequate child care is an important support that helps leavers stay at work. Although it is not a universal finding, most studies that examine the use of nonparental child care find that 80 percent or more of working leavers have someone watch their children. Interestingly, relatives and siblings are the most common sources of child care for working leavers; this option is likely a low- or no-cost one. Although working leavers may be eligible for child care subsidies if they are paying for care, only an average of one out of every five working leavers paying for care actually receive government support.

Finally, while food stamps and Medicaid can help improve the material well-being of working leavers, which should help them stay at work and off welfare, participation in these two programs is quite modest.

Notes

1. Some of this decline may be due to leavers "dropping out" of state UI data because they have moved across state lines. In two studies, employment rates actually dropped noticeably. Georgia reports a modest decline in employment rates from 64 to 57 percent between the first and fourth post-exit quarters; Iowa shows a substantial decline from 57 to 38 percent.
2. Alternatively, it is possible that continuous leavers have simply disappeared from administrative records, for example, by leaving the state. Since such leavers would not be present in either the state's TANF rolls or in its UI records, they will appear to be jobless continuous leavers.
3. Leavers who work in each of their first four post-exit quarters have not necessarily worked for the same employer or even been continuously employed over the year. They have, however, earned some money in each of the four quarters; leavers excluded from this group have experienced at least 13 consecutive weeks without working in a UI-covered job.
4. South Carolina, Illinois, and Iowa include some information about child care quality and parental satisfaction with child care arrangements.
5. The District of Columbia and Massachusetts also report child care arrangements used by employed leavers, but the categories of care reported make it difficult

to compare these studies with the others. Their findings are excluded from this discussion.

6. To facilitate comparisons across studies, we computed the share of children in each type of care arrangement out of all children in nonparental care.

7. Working leavers may have insurance through other sources, such as a former spouse, and their children may be eligible for and receive coverage through State Children's Health Insurance Programs.

5

Leaving Welfare But Not for Work

The previous chapters have shown that a large number of former welfare recipients are working. In this chapter, we examine the circumstances of those who are not working, in particular those who are not making successful transitions off of welfare.

Working is not the only measure of a successful transition for leavers. Indeed, not all nonworking leavers are facing difficulties. Some former recipients are married or cohabiting and rely on the earnings of partners. Others receive disability benefits, such as SSI or Social Security Disability Insurance (SSDI), which generally provide higher benefits than TANF.

Some leavers, however, are not able to make it off of TANF. Some return to welfare a relatively short time after exiting. A significant proportion has neither earned income from other family members nor cash income from government programs.

National data from the NSAF illustrate the relative size of groups of leavers by work and benefit status. Figure 5.1 categorizes all who left TANF between 1997 and 1999 by work, TANF, and disability benefit status at the time they were interviewed in 1999. Almost half of leavers were working and not receiving TANF benefits. An additional 2 percent were receiving disability benefits.[1] Other leavers, 9 percent, had a spouse or cohabiting partner who was working. Still others had worked recently (7 percent within the past three to eight months) and thus might be between jobs or have a greater potential to find a new job. About one-third of leavers were neither working nor receiving disability benefits. Twenty-two percent of leavers did not make a permanent transition off welfare and were back on TANF, and 12 percent of leavers were without any recent work experience. This group was disconnected from both the labor market and the TANF program—these leavers had no income from earnings, either their own or a partner's, were not on disability benefits, and were not receiving TANF.

In this chapter, we discuss the circumstances of those leavers whose transition off welfare has been less successful. We first examine the reasons leavers are not working and some of the key barriers to

Figure 5.1 Work and Benefit Status in 1999 Among All TANF Leavers 1997–1999

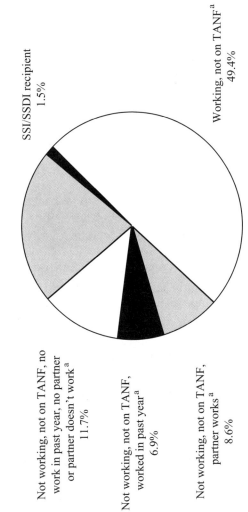

TANF recipient
21.9%

SSI/SSDI recipient
1.5%

Working, not on TANF[a]
49.4%

Not working, not on TANF, no
work in past year, no partner
or partner doesn't work[a]
11.7%

Not working, not on TANF,
worked in past year[a]
6.9%

Not working, not on TANF,
partner works[a]
8.6%

[a] Excludes SSI/SSDI recipients.
SOURCE: Data from the NSAF 1999.

work they report. We then examine the circumstances of nonworking leavers, including those who end up returning to welfare and those disconnected from the labor market and welfare programs. Among these two groups are many who left welfare involuntarily because they were sanctioned for failure to follow program requirements. We also examine whether these sanctioned families tend to be in worse economic circumstances than other leaver families.

REASONS FOR NOT WORKING

As we have already shown, a majority of former recipients in most study areas work at some point during the first four quarters after leaving. But these figures also indicate a substantial group, one-third to one-half, is not working at a given point in time after exit. Some of these former recipients are in and out of work, facing the issues of job retention discussed previously. A sizeable group, ranging from one-quarter to one-third of former recipients in most areas, has not worked in the year since exit. Because work is a key goal of the reform legislation and the predominant source of income for most low-income families, it is important to understand why such a large number of former recipients are not working.

The reasons former recipients are not working are varied and range from staying home to care for family to poor health or lack of necessary supports, such as child care and transportation. Several state studies and the NSAF report the main reason former recipients are not working at the time they were interviewed (typically 12 months after exit). Table 5.1 shows results for former recipients in the District of Columbia, Iowa, Missouri, New York, South Carolina, Washington, and the nation. The District of Columbia and South Carolina allow respondents to give multiple answers, resulting in comparatively higher percentages in these areas.

One of the most common reasons former recipients give for not working is taking care of family. This reason includes reports of a desire to stay home with children, pregnancy, and caring for an ill parent or child. Reports of this reason range from 14 percent in Iowa to 31 percent in Missouri. Nationally, 33 percent report they are not working because they are taking care of home or family. In addition,

Table 5.1 Reasons for Not Working for Leavers Who Are Not Currently Working

Reason	DC[a]	Iowa	Missouri	New York	South Carolina[a]	Washington	United States
				Percent reporting reason for not working			
Family[b]	26	14	31	26	21	21	33
In school/training	5	11	9	9	6	7	8
Poor health	17	23	26	17	24	17	29
Can't find a job	26	16	14	3	15	6	12
Laid off/fired	—	—	—	17	14	18	4
Lack child care	20	13	4	10	15	3	4
Lack transportation	9	6	6	2	13	1	2
Other[c]	19	17	9	15	9	25	9

NOTE: — = not available.

[a] Respondents allowed to give multiple answers.

[b] Includes wanting to stay home with children, pregnancy, caring for family, and health of other family members.

[c] Other includes did not want/need to work, retired, doing something else, lack skills, and in jail/treatment.

SOURCE: Based on survey data from leaver studies. U.S. data from NSAF 1999. See Table A.3 for a complete listing of the leaver studies cited.

close to a tenth of former recipients across these studies and in the nation report they are not working because they are in school or training.[2] For many former recipients, not working is a voluntary choice, indicating they do not need to rely on their own earnings while engaged in alternative activities. However, for some it may reflect the inability to find alternate care for ill or disabled family members.

Other reasons given for not working indicate recipients face serious barriers to work. A common reason leavers give for not working is that they are in poor health. About a quarter of former recipients in Iowa, Missouri, and South Carolina report health as the main reason they are not working. Nationally, 29 percent of former recipients said they were ill or disabled and unable to work. While these studies do not usually identify the specific health issue or its severity, other research shows high levels of serious mental health problems, including major depression, posttraumatic stress disorder, and generalized anxiety disorder, among former recipients (Danziger et al. 2000). Despite the high numbers of recipients reporting they aren't working for health reasons, most state studies report that only about 10 percent of all leavers are receiving federal disability benefits, either SSI or SSDI (Acs and Loprest 2001a). Nationally, 7 percent of former recipients who are not working and not back on TANF report receiving SSI/SSDI.[3] Only those with the most severe disabilities are likely to qualify for these benefit programs.

Leavers also report inability to find a job as their main reason for not working. Despite low national unemployment rates at the time these studies were conducted, inability to find a job was the main reason for not working given nationally by 12 percent of respondents in 1999. In specific area studies the numbers vary substantially from only 3 percent in New York to 16 percent in Iowa. Over a quarter of former recipients in the District of Columbia report they could not find a job, but this figure likely reflects respondents giving multiple reasons for not working. This variation may reflect differences in regional labor markets. In addition to inability to find a job, several studies recorded the numbers of respondents answering they were laid off or fired. While these are reasons for leaving a previous job, the high numbers citing these reasons indicate serious labor market issues and possibly difficulties finding a new job.[4]

Lack of child care or transportation are also reasons for not working, although the extent of these problems varies across areas. For example, in Iowa 13 percent of unemployed former recipients report lack
of child care as a reason for not working, while in Washington and
Missouri the percentage is only 3 and 4 percent, respectively. In the
District of Columbia, the percentage is higher (20 percent) but, again,
this reason may be one of many for not working. Nationally, 4 percent
of recipients reported lack of child care and 2 percent reported lack of
transportation as the main reason they are not working. Child care and
transportation problems could be more common barriers to employment than reflected here if they are not the main reason for not working,
but a contributing factor.

RETURNING TO WELFARE

For some recipients who exit TANF, the transition is not permanent. A substantial group of former recipients return to the cash assistance rolls. While past research has shown that there were families
cycling on and off cash assistance before welfare reform (Pavetti 1993)
and the extent of this cycling may not have increased after reform
(Bavier 2002), returning to cash assistance takes on increased urgency
in light of the lifetime limits on benefit receipt under TANF.

A sizeable minority of TANF leavers return to cash assistance in
the first year after leaving. From a fifth to a third of all leavers returned
to TANF at some point in the year following exit (Table 5.2).[5] Information from the NSAF supports these findings. Nationally, 22 percent of
those who had left welfare at some point between 1997 and 1999 were
back on TANF at the time they were interviewed in 1999.

In many areas, fairly steady TANF participation rates in the second
through fourth quarters after exit mask a fair degree of "cycling"—
families returning to TANF and then leaving again. In all of the studies
reporting TANF receipt at any point in the year after exit, a higher
percentage of leavers had returned to TANF over the course of the
year than are on it in the fourth quarter—in most cases a much higher
percentage. This finding indicates a large degree of movement off and
on TANF. For example, Wisconsin reports that 36 percent of leavers in
the study cohort return to TANF over the year after exit, but only 20

Table 5.2 Percent of Leavers Returning to TANF

State/study	Exit cohort	Receiving TANF in quarter relative to exit				Receipt any time in year after exit
		Q1	Q2	Q3	Q4	
Arizona[a]	1Q98	5	15	21	20	28
District of Columbia[a]	4Q98	7	13	17	19	21
Florida[b]	2Q97	7	14	13	11	25
Georgia	1Q98	3	10	14	14	22[c]
Illinois[b]	3Q97–4Q98	16	19	18	16	29
Iowa[a]	2Q99	6	15	22	24	30
Massachusetts	Dec. 1998–March 1999	3[d]	11	16	16	19
Missouri	4Q96	13	18	21	21	29
New York	1Q97	–	–	–	19	–
South Carolina	Oct. 1998–March 1999	3	9	12	11	17
Washington	4Q97	8	14	16	16	23
Wisconsin	4Q97	19	22	22	20	36
Cuyahoga County	3Q98	21	24	25	25	38
Bay Area	4Q98	19	21	23	–	–

NOTE: — = not available.

[a] Authors' calculations from leaver study data files.

[b] Data for month after exit, not quarter.

[c] Results for all who exited in 1998.

[d] Q1 statistic is for the third month after exit.

SOURCE: Based on administrative data from leaver studies. See Table A.3 for a complete listing of the leaver studies cited.

percent were on TANF in the fourth quarter after leaving. This finding means almost half of those who return to TANF at some point in the year after we first observe their exit have left again before the fourth quarter.

Evidence suggests that, nationally, returns to welfare are higher among those with significant barriers to work and lower among those receiving transitional support services (Loprest 2002b). Leavers with low education levels, little past work experience, and poor health have much higher rates of return to welfare than other leavers. However, those receiving subsidized child care, public health insurance, or government help with expenses are significantly less likely to return to welfare. Similar results were found for those receiving food stamps or Medicaid in Illinois (Lee, Lewis, and Stevens 2001).

NOT WORKING, NOT ON TANF

Among former TANF recipients who are not working, one group is of particular concern—those who do not have another worker in the family and do not have income from disability benefits or TANF. Essentially, these families are disconnected from the labor market and government cash assistance programs. While there are other sources of support such as child support, these families lack a major source of income that most former recipient families rely on. Some of these families may be on the verge of returning to welfare.

Figure 5.1 shows that 19 percent of former recipients fall into this "disconnected" category nationally—7 percent with some recent work experience and 12 percent without any recent work experience. The percentage of former recipients that are disconnected from work and welfare (calculated similarly) in four state studies show sizeable numbers of leavers in this situation across geographic areas. Table 5.3 shows that about one-fifth of leavers are not on TANF, not currently working, not living with a working spouse/partner, and not receiving disability benefits. This group ranges in size from 14 percent in Iowa to 21 percent in Arizona and the District of Columbia.

Because work among this population can be relatively unstable, it is possible that a number of these leavers are simply between jobs; that is, they have recently worked and will find another job soon. While

Table 5.3 Leavers Off TANF and Not Working

State/study	Percent of all leavers off TANF, not working, spouse not working, no SSI/SSDI[a]		
	Not currently working	Not recently worked[b]	No work since exit
Arizona[c]	21	—	9
DC[c]	21	—	10
Iowa[c]	14	—	6
New Jersey	18	13	—
United States	19	12	—

NOTE: — = not available.

[a] Includes leavers who are not receiving TANF at the time of the interview, and are also not working, do not have a working spouse or cohabiting partner, and are not receiving SSI or SSDI disability benefits.

[b] In New Jersey, "recent" is defined as past three months. In NSAF, "recent" is defined as in the year of the interview, which ranges from three to eight months.

[c] Arizona, DC, and Iowa figures are authors' calculations from leaver study data files.

SOURCE: Based on survey data from leaver studies. U.S. figures from NSAF (1999). See Table A.3 for a complete listing of the leaver studies cited. Results for New Jersey from Rangarajan and Wood (2000).

recent work does not completely predict future work or preclude serious hardship while unemployed, it is important to consider recent workers separately from those who have not recently worked or not worked at all since exiting TANF. The latter group is likely most vulnerable to being without a steady source of income. Table 5.3 shows that about 10 percent of all leavers in Arizona and the District of Columbia and 6 percent in Iowa are disconnected leavers and have not worked at all since exit. The percentage that has not recently worked is somewhat higher. In New Jersey, as in the national data, about 13 percent of all leavers had not recently worked and were off TANF.[6]

Not surprisingly, characteristics and circumstances that inhibit work are prevalent among these disconnected families (Loprest 2002a). Nationally, half of these families are in poor physical or mental health (Figure 5.2), which is significantly more than the 30 percent of working former recipients in poor health. Almost half (47 percent) last worked more than three years prior to the survey interview. More than a third (38 percent) have less than a high school education, and 8 percent have a child under age 1. Almost one-fifth have a child with a disability who receives SSI, compared with 5 percent of working former recipients. The difficulty of caring for a disabled child and finding child care can

68

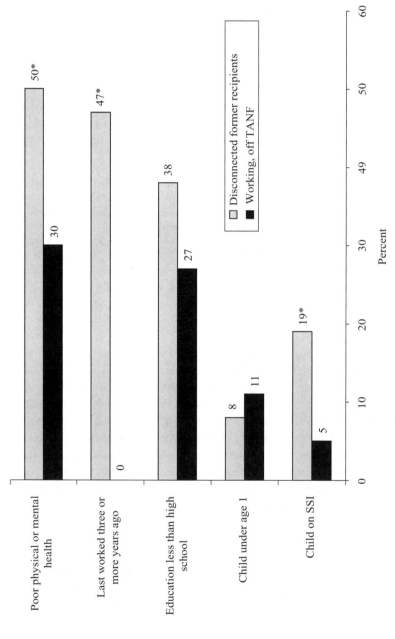

Figure 5.2 Potential Barriers to Work among Working, Disconnected and Working Former TANF Recipients, 1999

Poor physical or mental health — 50* / 30

Last worked three or more years ago — 47* / 0

Education less than high school — 38 / 27

Child under age 1 — 8 / 11

Child on SSI — 19* / 5

☐ Disconnected former recipients
■ Working, off TANF

Percent

0   10   20   30   40   49   50   60

NOTE: *Indicates two groups are significantly different at 90% significance level.
SOURCE: NSAF (1999).

make finding and keeping work more difficult. The child's SSI benefit, however, may be a major source of income for these families. A similar high incidence of these and other work barriers was documented in nonworking, non-TANF families in Michigan (Danziger et al. 2000).

In addition, these disconnected welfare leavers experience acute economic hardships. The incomes of these families are much lower than other former recipient families. The estimated median monthly income in 1999 from NSAF data is $210 compared with $1,390 for former welfare families with some earnings.[7] Even including the dollar value of food stamps for those who report receiving this benefit, monthly income only increases to around $530. While these estimates miss some sources of income, such as financial help from families and friends, the contrast is stark. New Jersey reports similar low income levels for a similarly defined group, about $500 monthly, with about half coming from family and friends (Rangarajan and Wood 2000).

Interestingly, follow-up study of this disconnected group in New Jersey, made possible by four annual surveys finds that, while a significant number fall into this group at the time of at least one of the four surveys (3 in 10), fewer than 4 in 10 of the disconnected were in the same situation 12 months later. Only about 5 percent of the original group of leavers remain disconnected for a year or more (Wood and Rangarajan 2003). This reflects both the possibility of reconnection for families, particularly movement back on to TANF, and the tenuousness of staying in a state of extreme impoverishment for a year. That relatively few families remain with virtually no steady source of income for more than a year is not surprising. That a substantial number of leavers and their children are ever in this situation is worthy of attention.

SANCTIONED LEAVERS

Under the Personal Responsibility and Work Opportunity Reconciliation Act of 1996 (PRWORA), states were required to impose at least partial benefit sanctions on welfare recipients that did not meet work or child support reporting requirements. Thirty-six states include in their programs the strictest possible sanction: a full-family sanction that takes away the entire TANF benefit.[8] In addition, families lose benefits for failing to follow rules, such as missing a recertification appointment or not providing necessary paperwork, but welfare offices consider them administrative terminations, not formal sanctions. Evidence suggests that this second group is even larger than those terminated for formal sanctions (Cherlin et al. 2001).

Families that leave welfare under either of these circumstances may not comply with rules because they no longer need or want benefits. Other families fail to follow the rules because they do not understand requirements or have problems that make compliance difficult, such as poor health or no access to child care. When families are terminated from the TANF program, it is difficult for agencies to maintain contact to assess hardship or to try to bring families back into compliance, although some states have made strides in these efforts (Pavetti, Derr, and Hesketh 2003). It is important to understand more about whether these families understood program rules, had the capacity to meet these rules, and how they survive once off welfare.

In most state studies, a small but significant number of families report leaving welfare because they did not comply with program rules.[9] Results vary from 10 to 14 percent of families leaving for this reason, although Illinois reports a high of 32 percent. Nationally, in 1999, 14 percent of leaver families reported exiting for this reason.

There is limited information on the circumstances of families that left welfare due to sanction or the broader category of failure to follow program rules. Most evidence highlights that this is a heterogeneous group, likely reflecting that some families choose not to follow rules because they no longer want or need benefits while other families have trouble understanding the rules or barriers to complying. Despite this variation, a national review of results on sanctioned families (USGAO 2000) and the Arizona leaver study found that, on average, sanctioned families face greater barriers to work and experience more post-exit hardships than other former recipient families, such as those leaving for work or marriage. Barriers include physical and mental health problems as well as difficulty finding child care or transportation.

In addition, those leaving welfare because they didn't follow rules make up a disproportionate percentage of the nonworking, non-TANF leavers described above. Nationally, in 1999, 32 percent of former recipients that had no income from earnings or TANF said they left welfare because of failure to follow program rules, compared with 13 percent for all leavers (Loprest 2002a). This group also has the highest rate of return to welfare among all the different reasons for leaving. This reflects in part families coming back into compliance after sanction and in part the difficult economic situation of some families cut from benefits because of failure to follow program rules.

SUMMARY

While many leaver families have gone to work, a significant number of leaver families have not made this transition and are facing economic hardships. Many leavers are not working because they are in poor health or cannot find a job. Some of this group has returned to TANF, thereby receiving income support, but again face the challenge of making a successful transition to work. About 10 to 15 percent of leavers are not working and have not returned to TANF. These disconnected leavers have significant barriers to work and are facing serious economic difficulties. The same is true for many of the families that left welfare involuntarily through sanction or failure to follow program rules.

Notes

1. The NSAF only collects information on disability benefit receipt for the year prior to the interview, so this may be an underestimate of SSI/SSDI receipt.
2. This does not include all former recipients who are in school because some combine work and school.
3. Reports of receipt are for the year prior to the interview. Because this figure does not include those who started to receive disability benefits in the year of the interview, it is likely an underestimate of the actual total.
4. This seems especially likely given the lower reports of inability to find a job in New York and Washington, which both report fairly high percentages laid off or fired, 17 and 18 percent, respectively.
5. Results for the first quarter after leaving are low in some studies due to the definitions used for leaver and for the first quarter after leaving. Most studies define a leaver as being off TANF for two months. If the first post-exit quarter includes these two months off welfare, return rates are likely lower for this quarter.
6. The survey data in Arizona, the District of Columbia, and Iowa did not allow for calculation of a comparable "not recently worked" number.
7. Current monthly income is estimated using NSAF data. It includes current monthly earnings of the former recipient and a spouse or partner as well as aver-

age monthly receipt from the previous year of child support payments, SSI, Social Security, pension, and investment income.

8. In 17 states, the full-family sanction is the immediate penalty for failure to meet work requirements. The other 19 states impose the full sanction only after multiple failures. Information is from the Urban Institute's Welfare Rules Database, 2000, which may be found at http://www.urban.org/Content/Research/Newfederalism/Data/ANFData.htm.

9. These findings are based on responses to survey questions. Survey results can vary dramatically from administrative data on exit reasons, mainly due to large numbers of welfare leavers never providing a reason for leaving to the TANF office. A comparison of survey and administrative reasons for leaving for these studies can be found in Acs and Loprest (2001a).

6
Family Well-Being

Income is a key indicator of economic well-being. Total family income measures the resources available to meet family needs. Leavers' earnings are a large part of income, but earnings of other family members, government benefits, and additional funds such as child support also play important roles. Further, comparing leavers' family income with the federal poverty level provides context for interpreting their relative well-being.

In addition to income, family well-being can be understood through former recipients' experiences of material hardships, such as problems with food, housing, and medical care. Many leaver studies collect information on these factors. Although there is no single benchmark comparison for these measures of hardship, examining former recipients' experiences of hardship before and after leaving welfare provides information on changes in well-being after exit.

In this chapter, we examine leaver families' income levels, income relative to poverty, and sources of income. We then discuss their experiences of food-related problems, housing problems, and lack of access to medical care. Given the emphasis in welfare reform discussions on success through work, we also discuss the relative well-being of working former recipient families compared with families where the leaver is not working. Along with these objective indicators, we also report former recipients' answers to direct questions of whether they are better off since leaving welfare.

FAMILY INCOME AND POVERTY

Family income is a powerful indicator of the well-being of welfare leavers. Not all leaver studies fully examine income because it is difficult to measure accurately. Most information on income comes from survey data, but to obtain accurate family income information, a survey must devote a great deal of time asking about each possible source of income and obtaining amounts. Even the leaver studies that do ask about income vary in the time and detail they devote to obtaining income data. We report results from nine leaver studies and the NSAF.

The variation in income levels across geographic areas is large. For example, mean monthly incomes range from $1,054 in Illinois to $1,601 in New York (Table 6.1).[1] This implies a difference of more than $6,500 a year in the incomes of leavers in these two states. Median incomes tend to be $200 to $300 lower. An estimate of leavers' income for the nation, excluding families that were back on welfare, falls somewhere in the middle of these results, with median monthly income of $1,151 in 1999 (Loprest 2002a). In general, leaver studies find that the incomes of families that left welfare and did not return are higher than the incomes of families that returned.

Several important differences across the studies likely affect reported incomes. Surveys that ask more detailed questions about income sources, such as Missouri's survey, will probably find higher average incomes than those that simply ask respondents to estimate their monthly incomes in a single question like the surveys for the District of Columbia and Illinois. Studies that ask about income a few months after exit are likely to find lower incomes than studies that ask about income one or two years after exit, assuming earnings growth over time. However, the pattern in these reported studies is not clear: Missouri reports average income higher more than two years after exit than many other state studies, but so do both Washington and the Bay Area less than a year after exit.

Income differences may also reflect differences in the cost of living. Consequently, it is not surprising to see high average incomes for New York and the Bay Area; however, the average incomes in Iowa and Missouri are also high, though the cost of living in Iowa is far lower than in California's Bay Area counties. The differences we observe likely are a combination of differences in study methods and true differences across geographic areas.

For the most part, these income figures are based on monthly cash income. This excludes food stamps, an important source of support for many of these families.[2] For example, a single mother with two children and a full-time minimum-wage job could receive $260 per month in food stamps. The difference food stamps can make in leaver family incomes can be seen in the national NSAF data. In 1999, median monthly income

Table 6.1 Monthly Income and Poverty of Welfare Leavers

State/study	Exit cohort	Timing of survey	Monthly income[a] ($) Mean	Median	Poverty level (%) <100% FPL	<185% FPL
Arizona	1Q98	12–18 months	1,361[b]	1,195	—	—
District of Columbia	4Q98	~12 months	1,091	800	—	—
Illinois	Dec. 98	6–8 months	1,054	895	—	—
Iowa	2Q99	8–12 months	1,440	—	47	80
Missouri	4Q98	26–34 months	1,427	1,166	58	89
New York	March/April 99	16–26 months	1,601	1,343	50	—
Washington	Oct. 98	6–8 months	1,208	1,000	58	—
Cuyahoga County	3Q98	14–21 months	1,169[c]	—	57[c]	—
Bay Area	4Q98	6–12 months	—	1,400	—	—
United States	1997–1999	1999	—	1,151[d]	53	—

NOTE: FPL = federal poverty level; — = not available.

[a] Income data are reported for households in Illinois and Missouri, families in Arizona and Washington, and for welfare cases in all other studies.

[b] Authors' calculations from Arizona leaver study data files removing the value of food stamps based on the average percent of family income from food stamps in Arizona.

[c] Includes cash value of food stamps.

[d] Estimate of monthly income at the time of the interview.

SOURCE: Based on survey data from leaver studies. U.S. data from NSAF 1999. See Table A.3 for a complete listing of the leaver studies cited.

for all leaver families increased from $1,151 to $1,449, or by 25 percent, when the estimated value of food stamps was included for families that reported receiving this benefit. Arizona and Iowa also report higher average incomes when including the value of food stamps.

Comparison of the percent of leaver families with income below the federal poverty level to the percent of all U.S. families with income below this level gives us a sense of how leaver family incomes compare with all U.S. families. Five of the nine studies report information on income relative to poverty for leaver families.[3] In Missouri, Washington, and Cuyahoga County, over half of all single-parent leavers are poor (Table 6.1). In Iowa and New York, roughly half of all leaver families are poor. Nationwide, 53 percent of families that are not back on welfare are poor. In comparison, in 2000, 8.6 percent of all U.S. families were poor (Dalaker 2001). Including the cash value of food stamp benefits reduces the percentage of leavers who are poor. For the nation, the percent poor falls from 53 to 41 percent. Similarly, the poverty rate for Iowa's leavers drops from 47 percent to 41 percent.

Iowa and Missouri also report the share of leavers who have incomes below 185 percent of the federal poverty level. Above this level of income, most families become ineligible for virtually all low-income support programs, including the EITC; this cutoff is a rough marker for self-sufficiency. In Iowa, only one out of five leavers have incomes above 185 percent of the federal poverty level. In Missouri, about 1 out of 10 leavers have incomes above this threshold.

Changes in Income after Exit

None of the leaver studies we examine here collects enough information to ascertain differences in family income before and after leaving welfare. While it is difficult to accurately measure income levels, it is even more difficult to obtain a measure of change in income over time. Collecting this type of information in one survey would require respondents to recall detailed income sources and amounts for two separate time periods, which would likely be confusing and inaccurate.

Data from longitudinal studies which survey recipients before and after leaving welfare, have been used to provide information on changes in leaver families' income. Bavier (2001), using SIPP data, finds that about half of the families that left welfare after 1996 experienced a drop in income. Repeated cross-section surveys, including the Current Population Survey and the NSAF, have also been used to examine changes in income of single-parent families with children with similar results. Zedlewski (2002) finds an increase in average incomes for single-parent families between 1996 and 1998 but a decline in incomes for the poorest fifth of single-parent families. In a slightly different take on the question, Danziger et al. (2002) study the net gains of moving from welfare to work using longitudinal surveys of welfare recipients in a Michigan county. They find that, for those moving from welfare to work, monthly net income increased by $2.63 for every additional hour of work.

The Washington study uses an alternative method to assess the change in income before and after exit. This study compares the incomes and poverty rates of TANF leavers with those of families still on TANF. Because the composition of the remaining group of TANF recipients differs from leavers, this is not the same as measuring the change in income of leavers. However, it does provide insight into differences in the circumstances of these two groups. The Washington study finds that although 58 percent of Washington's leavers are poor, a much higher percentage (86 percent) of families receiving TANF have incomes that fall below the poverty level. This shows that, although leavers have low incomes, on average they do better than those remaining on welfare.

Sources of Income

Because the majority of leavers are working, it is not surprising to find that earnings from work is the most common source of income for leaver families. However, many leaver families are also receiving income from other sources, including earnings from other family members, child support, government disability benefits, food stamps, and help from family and friends. Table 6.2 reports the percent of leaver families that are receiving income from these sources as reported by nine leaver studies.

The majority of leaver families have some reliance on earnings as a form of income. Sixty to 70 percent have income from their own earnings. In addition, many leaver families have earnings from other family members. Five studies report the percent of leaver families that

Table 6.2 Percent of Leaver Families Receiving Various Sources of Income at Time of Interview

State/study	Exit cohort	Timing of survey post–exit	Own earnings	Other earnings	Any earnings	Child support	SSI	Social Security	Food stamps	Family/ friends
District of Columbia	4Q98	~12 months	60	—	64	11	12	—	41	11
Georgia	1Q99–2Q00	~6 months	69	—	—	—	—	—	74	59
Illinois	Dec. 98	6–8 months	63	—	66[a]	31[b]	12[c]	6[c]	33	14
Iowa	2Q99	8–12 months	60	37	—	28	7[c]	7[c]	43	25
Massachusetts	12/98–03/99	~12 months	71	16	77	46	20[c]	—	38	18
Missouri	4Q98	26–34 months	65	—	80	22	12	—	47	—
South Carolina[d]	12/98–03/99	12 months	61	—	67	26[e]	10	8	61	4[e]
Washington	Oct. 98	6–8 months	60	21	—	23	4	4	50[c]	—
Cuyahoga County	3Q98	14–21 months	69	21	—	13	5	—	—	12

Percent of leavers with income from

NOTE: — = not available.

[a] Head or spouse/partner only; other household members' earnings not included.

[b] For cases with an absent parent.

[c] Percent receiving source at some point since exit.

[d] Results are for families that remain off of welfare at the time of the survey.

[e] Percent with this income as primary source of support.

SOURCE: Based on survey data from leaver studies. See Table A.3 for a complete listing of the leaver studies cited.

have earnings from any family member, with reports ranging from 64 percent in the District of Columbia to 80 percent in Missouri.

Child support is another source of income for leaver families, since all of these families have children and many of them are single-parent families. In six out of the eight studies with information on receipt of child support, more than 20 percent of leavers report this source of income. In Massachusetts, however, nearly half of all leavers (46 percent) say they have some income from an absent parent.

Government benefits from disability programs and food stamps are also a source of income for a number of leaver families. From 4 to 20 percent of leaver families receive SSI for people with disabilities and between 4 and 8 percent of leaver families receive Social Security benefits.[4] Government food stamp benefits are a source of income for a third or more leaver families. Receipt ranges from 33 percent in Illinois to 74 percent in Georgia. This variation reflects differences in income levels, and therefore eligibility for food stamps, among leaver families. It also reflects differences in program outreach to leaver families about their continued eligibility for these benefits.

Finally, family and friends are a source of income support. There is a great deal of variation in the percentage of leaver families receiving this type of help across studies, ranging from 11 percent in the District of Columbia to 59 percent in Georgia. Interestingly, 4 percent of families in South Carolina report income from family and friends as their primary source of support.

The extent to which families receive these different sources of income does not provide a full picture of their reliance on each source. While relatively few families receive SSI income, it may be a large percentage of those families' income. One way to better understand the importance of different sources of income is to examine the share of total income from each source. This requires knowing the percentage of leaver families receiving a source and the amount of income received from each source. Unfortunately, few studies collect this level of information. Figure 6.1 shows results for three studies, Arizona, Iowa, and Washington, where we are able to calculate the share of leaver family income from each source, aggregated across all leaver families.[5] Thus, families with zero percent of income from a source are included as well as families with positive income from that source.

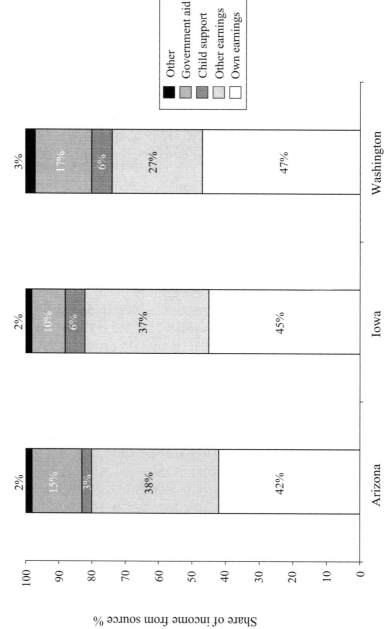

Figure 6.1 Share of Income, by Source, for All Leaver Families in Selected Studies (%)

SOURCE: Authors' calculations from leaver study survey data files.

Not only do the majority of leaver families have income from earnings, leavers' earnings are, on average, the major source of income for all leaver families in these states. Between 42 and 47 percent of family income comes from the earnings of leavers. The earnings of other family members are also a substantial source of income, accounting for an additional 27 to 38 percent of income. Income from child support plays a smaller role, with 3 to 6 percent of income coming from this source. This is in part because fewer families receive this source of support. Among families that receive child support, the percent of their income coming from this source is substantially higher, 28 percent in Arizona and 29 percent in Washington.

Government benefits, including TANF, SSI, Social Security, and other government programs, still account for a significant share of leaver families' incomes.[6] In Iowa, 10 percent of leaver family income is from government benefits. In Arizona and Washington, 15 and 17 percent of income is from these sources, respectively. These results reflect income between 6 and 12 months after exiting TANF and include those who have returned to TANF. Among those leavers with TANF income at the time of the interview, 45 to 50 percent of income (in Arizona and Missouri) was from TANF.

Income by Employment Status

Because earnings are the most important source of income for former recipients, we would expect incomes to be higher for workers than nonworkers. This holds true in the studies for which we have information on income by work status: Arizona, the District of Columbia, New York, and Washington (Table 6.3). The table shows mean and median incomes for those who are employed and those who are not employed at the time of the survey interview. We also show the incomes of families where the leaver has not worked at all since exiting TANF.[7]

In these studies, working leavers have monthly incomes far above the incomes of those who are not currently working. In the District of Columbia and Washington, median monthly income of currently employed leavers is more than double that of leavers who are not currently employed. New York reports that 63 percent of currently employed leavers' incomes are above the poverty level, compared with

Table 6.3 Monthly Income of Welfare Leavers, by Employment Status ($)

State/study	All leavers	Employment status		
		Currently employed	Not currently employed	Never worked since exit
Arizona[a,b]				
Mean	1,361	1,727	892	—
Median	1,195	1,400	720	—
District of Columbia				
Mean	1,091	1,353	675	647
Median	800	1,102	500	547
New York				
Mean	1,601	1,965	985[c]	954
Median	1,343	1,376	743[c]	600
Washington[a]				
Mean	1,227	1,462	870	884
Median	1,000	1,200	576	601

NOTE: — = not available.
[a] Authors' calculations from leaver study data files.
[b] Authors' calculations from Arizona leaver study data files removing the value of food stamps based on the average percent of family income from food stamps in Arizona.
[c] Includes those currently not working who have worked since leaving TANF.
SOURCE: Based on survey data from leaver studies. See Table A.3 for a complete listing of the leaver studies cited.

only 15 percent of families that are not currently working. These differences in income are huge.

In addition, some studies provide information separately on the incomes of leavers who never worked since leaving TANF (Table 6.3). Interestingly, the data show relatively small differences in the average incomes of those families where the leaver never worked since exit and those who are not currently employed. On the one hand, families where the leaver has never worked do not seem to have an alternate source of income that is pushing their incomes above those of the not currently employed. On the other hand, they are not in worse straights monetarily than those with some past work experience, at least in the current month. Given the importance of earnings in lifting leaver family incomes, if these families are not able to access work in the future, they may have a bleaker long-term picture than those not currently employed whose past work experience provides some prospect for future work.

Information on the sources of income for families that are not currently employed shows that a greater percentage of families where the leaver is not currently working rely on government aid as a source of income (Table 6.4). This includes families that have returned to welfare. For example, in Arizona, 26 percent of welfare leavers that are not currently employed receive TANF and 59 percent receive some other government aid. Among those currently employed, only 6 percent receive TANF and 35 percent receive government aid.[8] In addition, in these three studies (Arizona, Iowa, and Washington), a higher percentage of families where the leaver is not currently employed have earnings from other family members. In Iowa and Washington, a substantially higher percentage of working families than those not currently working receive child support.

EXPERIENCES OF MATERIAL HARDSHIP

Because income does not capture all aspects of family well-being, many studies have collected information on former recipients' experi-

Table 6.4 **Leaver Families with Select Sources of Income, by Employment Status**

| State/study | Percent receiving | | | |
	Other earnings	Child support	Government aid[a]	TANF
Arizona[b]				
Currently employed	29	17	35	6
Not currently employed	31	16	59	26
Iowa				
Currently employed	35	35	22	—
Not currently employed	46	17	56	—
Washington[b]				
Currently employed	20	26	17	—
Not currently employed	21	17	31	—
Never worked since exit	31	24	28	—

NOTE: — = not available.
[a] Government aid includes various public support programs such as SSI, SSDI, general assistance, UI, child care assistance, emergency assistance, and "other assistance." Arizona includes food stamps and Iowa includes TANF. Washington includes SSI, Social Security, general assistance, UI, retirement benefits, workers compensation, and "other assistance."
[b] Authors' calculations from leavers study data files.
SOURCE: Based on survey data from leaver studies. See Table A.3 for a complete listing of the leaver studies cited.

ences of material hardships, such as hunger, housing, and medical care problems. The addition of these measures significantly broadens our understanding of the well-being of welfare leavers.

Comparing the level of material hardship across studies is difficult because the survey questions used to ascertain material hardship vary from study to study, sometimes quite substantially.[9] Another complication for assessing hardship is the lack of a natural benchmark for comparison like the official poverty line is for income. Comparing former recipients' experience of hardship before and after leaving welfare is one way of putting these results in context, and we report these changes here. In addition, we report results from questions that directly ask former recipients if they are better off since leaving welfare.

Hunger and Food-Related Problems

One area of concern is the extent to which families that left welfare experience problems with the basic necessity of food. State studies use various measures to assess the extent and severity of food-related problems leaver families experience. Although measures differ across studies, most studies find that one-quarter to one-half of leaver families report some type of food-related problems.

One standard way to measure hunger is with the Household Food Security Scale developed by the USDA. Results for specific studies can be compared with national results using this measure. Three studies (Iowa, Massachusetts, and Cuyahoga County) report a measure of "food insecurity" based on answers to the six-item USDA scale. The scale includes questions on having to cut or skip meals, whether food lasts to the end of the month, and worrying about having enough food.[10] These studies also report the more severe situation of food insecurity with hunger (defined as answering yes to at least five out of the six questions on the USDA food insecurity scale).

In all three of these studies, about a third or more of leaver families (32 to 46 percent) report experiencing food insecurity (Table 6.5). Between 16 and 26 percent of leaver families experienced food insecurity with hunger between the time they left TANF and the time of the survey. This compares with the 10 percent of all U.S. households that reported being food insecure in 1998, including 4 percent that experience food insecurity with hunger. The level of food insecurity among

Table 6.5 Leaver Families' Experience of Food Insecurity

				Percent reporting problem	
Problem	IA	MA	Cuyahoga County	All U.S. households	All U.S. households <100% FPL
Food insecurity	32	43	46	10	35
Food insecurity with hunger	16	22	26	4	14

NOTE: FPL = federal poverty level.
SOURCE: Based on survey data from leaver studies. See Table A.3 for a complete listing of the leaver studies cited. Data for U.S. households from USDA (1999).

welfare leavers in these studies is more similar to that of all households with income below the poverty level. Of all poor households, 35 percent are food insecure and 14 percent experience food insecurity with hunger (USDA 1999).

Other studies report less standardized measures of whether leavers experienced various food-related problems, including not having enough to eat, not being able to afford food, food not lasting until the end of the month, or having to cut or skip meals. A large percentage of leaver families report experiencing at least one of these food-related problems in the time since exiting welfare (Table 6.6). Nationally, about a third of leaver families in 1999 report some experience of food hardship in the past year (Loprest 2001).

Seeking help from emergency food service providers, such as food banks or pantries, food kitchens or shelters, churches, or other charitable or community organizations, is another indication of food hardship. While the percentage of leaver families reporting they sought out these services varies, in four out of eight of the studies reporting these results, 20 percent or more of all leavers received emergency food services since exiting (Table 6.7).[11]

Housing-Related Hardships

Many leavers experience difficulty affording housing and utilities. Again, the surveys use various measures to assess the extent to which leavers are experiencing housing-related problems. Table 6.8 shows that, in all but one of the studies, between one-quarter and one-half of leaver families report having fallen behind on rent or housing costs. Nationally, 46 percent of leaver families in 1999 report that they had

Tabe 6.6 Leaver Families' Experience of Food-Related Problems

Problem				Percent reporting problem				
	AZ	DC	GA	IL	MO	SC[a]	WA	Bay Area
Cut size of meals or skipped meals (one or more months)		25		25		20	43/27[b]	
Almost every month		6				6		
Child cut or skipped meals					3		13/4[b]	
Food didn't last (often or sometimes)		46		44		53		
Food didn't last (often)		13				11		
Not enough to eat at times	24		13					31
Went without food all day at least once							15	
Could not afford balanced meals (often or sometimes)			18			38		
Is unable to buy enough food					26			
Ate less because not enough money						22		
Hungry but didn't eat because couldn't afford						10		
Worried food wouldn't last		53	38					

[a] Results are for families that remain off of welfare at the time of the survey.
[b] Cut size of meal/skipped meals are reported separately.
SOURCE: Based on survey data from leaver studies. See Table A.3 for a complete listing of the leaver studies cited.

Table 6.7 Leaver Families' Receipt of Emergency Food Services

					Percent reporting problem			
Problem	AZ	IL	IA	MA	MO[a]	SC[a,b]	WA	Cuyahoga County
Received emergency food services								
From religious, community, or charitable organization	12				7	2		10
From food pantry/food kitchen/shelters/food banks	21	12	28[c]	29		3	35	
Received food or $ for food from friends/relatives	21				7	14		

[a] Whether assistance was received was asked only of those who cut or skipped meals (SC) or were unable to buy enough food (MO). Numbers are authors' recalculations to represent the percentage of all leavers.

[b] Results are for families that remain off of welfare at the time of the survey.

[c] Results are for assistance from food pantry. Iowa also reports 3 percent receiving assistance from soup kitchens.

SOURCE: Based on survey data from leaver studies. See Table A.3 for complete listing of the leaver studies cited.

Table 6.8 Leaver Families' Experience of Difficulty Paying for Housing

Problem	Percent reporting problem								
	AZ	DC	GA	IL	IA	MO	SC[a]	WA	Cuyahoga County
Behind on rent/housing costs	37	27	18	38	25	26[b]	33		26
Forced to move because of housing costs	17	6					12		
Evicted			4					7	7[c]

[a] Results are for families that remain off of welfare at the time of the survey.
[b] Unable to pay rent, mortgages, or utilities.
[c] Percent reporting eviction, staying in emergency shelter, or homelessness.
SOURCE: Based on survey data from lever studies. See Table A.3 for a complete listing of the leaver study cited.

problems paying rent, mortgage, or utilities in the past year. Some families (6 to 26 percent) report they were forced to move because of housing costs, while a smaller percentage of leaver families (4 to 7 percent) report being evicted since exiting welfare.

Many studies also gather information on problems of access to housing (Table 6.9). A small percentage (generally 1 to 3 percent) of families report using a homeless shelter. About 10 percent of families report they did not have a place to live. An even higher share of leaver families report moving in with relatives or friends because of high housing costs or difficulty paying housing costs. Nationally, 9 percent of leavers report moving in with others because of difficulty paying mortgage, rent, or utility bills.

In addition to problems with rent and places to stay, a number of families had problems paying utilities or had utilities cut off because of failure to pay (Table 6.10). The percentage of families that were behind on utilities after leaving welfare ranges from 22 percent in Georgia to 48 percent in South Carolina. A smaller percentage report they had utilities turned off.

Access to Medical Care

Some leaver families also face the hardship of being unable to afford or access health care services. The extent of this problem varies

Table 6.9 Leaver Families' Experience of Problems with Access to Housing

Problem	Percent reporting problem						
	AZ	DC	IL	IA	MA	SC[a]	WA
Without a place to live at least once			1[b]	7			13
Used homeless shelter	3	3	3		2[c]	2	1
Did not have own place to live					8		
Moved in with family/friends		22	11		14		10

[a] Results are for families that remain off of welfare at the time of the survey.
[b] Only asked of respondents who had moved at least once since exit. Number is authors' recalculation to represent the percentage of all leavers.
[c] Lived in a car or on the streets.
SOURCE: Based on survey data from leaver studies. See Table A.3 for a complete listing of the leaver studies cited.

Table 6.10 Leaver Families' Experience of Difficulty Paying Utilities

							Percent reporting problem		
Problem	AZ	DC	GA	IL	IA	MA	SC[a]	WA	Cuyahoga County
Behind on utility payments		29	22				48		
Utilities turned off/went without	12			14		26			
Heat		5			8		9		
Electricity		6	12[b]		7		11	12[b]	19[b]
Water		3					7		

[a] Results are for families that remain off of welfare at the time of the survey.
[b] Results include both gas and electricity.
SOURCE: Based on survey data from leaver studies. See Table A.3 for a complete listing of the leaver studies cited.

across areas (Table 6.11). In Illinois and Cuyahoga County, a third or more families report not getting medical attention when needed, while 10 percent of families in Georgia and South Carolina had this problem.

MATERIAL HARDSHIP BY EMPLOYMENT STATUS

Despite the higher incomes of leavers who are currently employed (shown earlier), work-related expenses or loss of other government benefits, such as Medicaid and food stamps, could exacerbate material hardship. Leaver studies find that, generally, material hardship is lower for working families.[12] The Iowa, Illinois, and South Carolina studies find that leavers who are working have lower levels of food, housing, and health care related problems than those who are not working (Table 6.12). In addition, in Missouri those currently employed have fewer experiences of food and housing hardships when compared with leavers who have never worked. There is variation in the degree of difference between employed and not employed leavers across these studies. Illinois shows the most marked differences in hardships between working and nonworking families. For example, 55 percent of unemployed leavers in Illinois could not afford food compared with 38 percent of employed leavers, and 54 percent of unemployed leavers were behind on rent compared with 29 percent of employed leavers.

Changes in Material Hardships Since Exit

Comparing experiences of material hardship before and after leaving welfare gives an indication of whether well-being increased or de-

Table 6.11 Leaver Families' Experience of Difficulty Receiving Health Care

	Percent reporting problem					
Problem	AZ	DC	GA	IL	SC[a]	Cuyahoga County
Could not afford health care	24	8				
Did not get medical attention when needed			10	31	10	40

[a] Results are for families that remain off of welfare at the time of the survey.
SOURCE: Based on survey data from leaver studies. See Table A.3 for a complete listing of the leaver studies cited.

Table 6.12 Leavers' Experience of Material Hardship, by Employment Status

	DC		IA		IL		MO			SC[a]	
	\#\#\#										

Percent reporting problem

Problem	DC Emp.	DC Not emp.	IA Emp.	IA Not emp.	IL Emp.	IL Not emp.	MO Emp.	MO Not emp.	MO No emp. since exit	SC[a] Emp.	SC[a] Not emp.
Food-related hardships											
Cut the size of meals or skipped meals (all or some months)	25	26			21	32	2[b]	4[b]	8[b]	17	25
Could not afford food/food didn't last (often or sometimes)	47	44			38	55	25[c]	26[c]	26[c]		
Food insecurity			29	40							
Housing-related hardships											
Behind on rent/housing costs	28	27	25	25	29	54	21[d]	37[d]	25[d]	31	35
Behind on utility payments	33	24	34	46						48	49
Went without utilities	5[e]	6[e]	4[f]	11[f]	12	17				10[e]	14[e]
Used homeless shelter	1	6			1	7				2	3
Medical-care hardships											
Did not get medical care when needed	8	9			25	39				8	14

[a] Results are for families that remain off of welfare at the time of the survey.
[b] Child skipped meal due to lack of food.
[c] Unable to buy enough food.
[d] Unable to pay rent, mortgage, or utilities.
[e] Went without electricity.
[f] Were ever homeless.
SOURCE: Based on survey data from leaver studies. See Table A.3 for a complete listing of the leaver studies cited.

creased after exit. Five studies compare material hardship experiences before and after exit based on the respondents' recollection at the time of interview.[13] In addition, the Washington study compares leavers with a separate sample of families still on TANF. Tables 6.13 and 6.14 provide a subset of measures pre- and post-exit for food, housing, and health care hardships. Unfortunately, most of the reports from which these results are drawn do not discuss whether differences pre- and post-exit are statistically significant, so we cannot include this information in our discussion here. Instead, we focus on the largest differences and whether there exist patterns of change across the multiple measures.

Across the variety of measures used to assess material hardships, study results vary on whether hardships increased after exiting TANF. In Massachusetts and South Carolina, leavers report increases in hardship across most measures of problems with food, housing, and medical care. In Arizona and Illinois, there is a general decline in food and housing hardships after leaving TANF, but an increase in difficulties accessing medical care. In the District of Columbia and Washington, the results are mixed depending on the specific hardship measure. Interestingly, difficulties affording and accessing medical care increase in all five studies reporting on this hardship. This fits with the large declines in leavers' Medicaid coverage after exit.

OVERALL WELL-BEING

Leaver families in six studies are asked directly to compare their overall well-being since exiting TANF to a prior time when they were on TANF (Table 6.15). The specific questions vary, from asking about change in overall well-being to emotional well-being to general standard of living. Several studies report the percentage of families claiming they are better off, worse off, or the same relative to before leaving TANF, with two studies, Arizona and Washington, reporting finer gradations.

At least half of all families report they are better off since leaving welfare. More than two-thirds of families report they are better off in Arizona. South Carolina asks families whether they agree or disagree with the statement "Life was better when I was getting welfare," and

Table 6.13 Leavers' Experience of Food-Related Problems: Comparing Time before and after Exiting TANF

	Percent reporting problem									
	AZ		IL		MA		SC[a]		WA	
Problem	Pre	Post	Pre	Post	Pre	Post	Pre	Post	Caseload	Leavers
Food insecurity										
Food insecurity with hunger					30	43				
Cut the size of meals or skipped meals (one or more months)			24	25	14	22	14	20	39/22[b]	43/27[b]
Almost every month							3	6		
Child cut or skipped meals									16/5[b]	13/4[b]
Not enough to eat at times	30	24								
Food did not last (often or sometimes)			51	44						
Went without food all day at least once										
Unable to buy enough food									11	15
Ate less because not enough money							13	22		
Hungry but did not eat because couldn't afford							8	10		
Received emergency food services										
From religious, community, or charitable organization	15	12					2[c]	2[c]		
From food pantry/food kitchens/shelters/food banks	29	21	15	12	26	29	2[c]	3[c]	44	35
Received food/money for food from friends/relatives	24	21					9	14		

[a] Results for families that remain off of welfare at the time of the survey.

[b] Washington reports cut meal size/skipped meals separately.

[c] Whether assistance was received was asked only of those who cut or skipped meals. Numbers are authors' recalculations to represent the percentage of all leavers.

SOURCE: Based on survey data from leaver studies. See Table A.3 for a complete listing of the leaver studies cited.

Table 6.14 Leavers' Experience of Housing-Related and Medical Care Problems: Comparing Time before and after Exiting TANF

Problem	AZ		DC		IL		MA		SC[a]		WA	
	Pre	Post	Pre	Post	Pre	Post	Pre	Post	Pre	Post	Caseload	Leavers
Behind on rent/housing costs	41	37	27	27	45	38			25	33		
Forced to move because of housing costs	21	17	8	6	15	13			19	12		
Evicted					2[b]	1[b]					3	7
Without a place to live at least once	4	3	5	3	4	3					11	13
Used homeless shelter							2[c]	2[c]	3	2	2	1
Did not have own place to live							3	8				
Moved in with family/friends					14	11					7	10
Behind on utility payments	18	12	29	29					26	48		
Utilities turned off/went without					27	14	20	26				
Heat			7	5					6	9		
Electricity			7	6					9	12	12[d]	12[d]
Water			2	3					5	7		
Phone disconnected									23	35		
Could not afford health care	14	24	3	8					4	10		
Did not get medical attention					26	31						

[a] Results are for families that remain off of welfare at the time of the survey.
[b] Only asked of respondents who had moved at least once since exit. Numbers are authors' recalculations to reflect percentage of all leavers.
[c] Lived in a car on the streets.
[d] Results include both gas and electricity.
SOURCE: Based on survey data from leaver studies. See Table A.3 for a complete listing of the leaver studies cited.

Table 6.15 Overall Current Well-Being Relative to before Leaving TANF

State/study	Percent reporting well-being as				
	Much better off	Better off	Same	Worse off	Much worse off
Arizona	31	37	16	12	3
Illinois[a]	n/a	57	30	13	n/a
Iowa[a,b]	n/a	49	32	19	n/a
Massachusetts[a,c]	n/a	47	26	28	n/a
South Carolina[d]	n/a	80	n/a	20	n/a
Washington	32	28	19	13	8

NOTE: n/a = not applicable.
[a] Respondents were asked only whether "better off," "same," or "worse off."
[b] Current standard of living relative to before exit.
[c] Emotional well-being relative to before leaving TANF. Numbers for financial well-being are similar.
[d] Respondents were asked to agree or disagree with the statement, "Life was better when I was getting welfare."
SOURCE: Based on survey data from leaver studies. See Table A.3 for a complete listing of the leaver studies cited.

80 percent disagree. Approximately one-fifth or fewer of families report they are worse off or much worse off after leaving TANF than before in all states except Massachusetts, where 28 percent report they are worse off. Illinois has the lowest percentage of leavers who say they are worse off since leaving TANF (13 percent).

Interestingly, this overall self-assessment of relative well-being does not always accord with the leavers' reports of specific measures of hardship discussed earlier. For Arizona and Illinois, the relatively high percentage of leaver families reporting they are better off after exit matches the generally lower levels of specific food and housing hardships reported in these studies. However, the results for Massachusetts and South Carolina are not consistent. In these studies, the majority of families report they are not worse off since exiting, although the results on specific hardship measures show general increases in the experience of many types of food, housing, and medical care related hardships.

SUMMARY

In summary, while the average incomes of leavers vary across geographic areas, most leavers have low incomes. About two in five leaver families live in poverty. Measures of leavers' experience of food and housing related material hardships, while varied, show that about a quarter or more leaver families experience some of these problems after leaving TANF. Whether these problems are greater or lesser after exit varies across the state studies. A somewhat smaller percentage of leavers have trouble accessing medical care, but this problem generally increased after leaving TANF.

These results emphasize the importance of work for the well-being of leaver families. Earnings of a leaver or another member of the family is the primary source of income for leavers. Families without a worker have substantially lower incomes and generally face greater material hardships.

Notes

1. The income "unit" varies slightly across the studies. For example, Illinois and Missouri report household income, Washington reports family income, and Arizona presents case income.
2. Income for Cuyahoga County includes the cash value of food stamps.
3. Because income flows vary over the course of a year, especially earnings, average annual income cannot be measured accurately by multiplying average monthly income by 12.
4. Since the majority of leaver families would not yet be eligible for retirement benefits, receipt of Social Security benefits for these families is likely disability insurance benefits, survivor benefits, or a misreport of SSI benefits.
5. Reports are the authors' calculations from leaver studies' data files. See Chapter 2 for more details. Shares are computed by dividing average income for those with the source by average family income.
6. Because reporting was not done separately, Arizona includes food stamps in government aid and in total income.
7. This group is a subset of those not currently working in the District of Columbia and Washington and is mutually exclusive from the not currently employed group in New York.
8. Current workers can receive TANF if they are combining work and welfare.
9. Attempts have been made by government agencies such as USDHHS to encourage use of common measures such as the scale for food insecurity and hunger promulgated by USDA.
10. The complete and shortened scale can be found at USDA (1999).
11. Lower results for Missouri and South Carolina may represent conservative estimates because these states only ask the subset of leavers reporting a specific food problem these questions about seeking assistance.

12. Five studies allow for comparisons between employed leavers and those who are not employed. Missouri reports results separately for those who have worked at some point and those who never worked since exit. Illinois also reports separate results for those who are continuously employed, intermittently employed, and never employed since exit. We do not show these results here.

13. Arizona, Illinois, and Washington use a six-month window for their questions (e.g., "Have you experienced this problem in the past six months? Before the past six months?"). South Carolina uses a 12-month window. These windows roughly correspond to pre- and post-exit time periods. The District of Columbia and Massachusetts ask about the time while on TANF and the time since leaving TANF, about 10 months for Massachusetts and 12 months for the District of Columbia. All of these studies compare leavers' experiences before and after exit except for Washington.

7
Conclusion

For more than half a century, the federal government provided cash assistance to low-income families with children through AFDC. All families that met eligibility requirements were entitled to financial assistance. Critics of this entitlement program charged that it destroyed the incentive to work, discouraged marriage, and promoted nonmarital childbearing and long-term dependence on government assistance. Although some of these criticisms were exaggerated, by the early 1990s, public disenchantment with AFDC reached such high levels that the program was no longer sustainable.

Gradually, under waivers to federal program rules, states began imposing new requirements on recipients. Finally, in 1996, Congress and President Clinton scrapped the old federal entitlement program and replaced it with the TANF block grant. With this landmark end to entitlement came a lifetime limit on the receipt of welfare benefits. Further, recipients face increasingly strict requirements, such as mandated participation in work activities, as a condition of receiving aid. Noncompliance with these requirements can lead to severe financial penalties, including termination of assistance.

All these changes made welfare less attractive to would-be recipients. Other policy changes increased the relative attractiveness of work compared to welfare. Many states allowed families with jobs to keep more of their earnings, making it easier to combine work and welfare. Additional funds were made available to reduce the cost of child care. And the EITC program expanded considerably, creating a credit of up to $4,140 for a family with two children in 2002.

These changes occurred in the mid to late 1990s, a period marked by sustained economic growth. Both poverty and unemployment fell to their lowest levels in three decades.

Against this backdrop, millions of families left welfare. Studies of the families that left welfare in this post-entitlement era document the experiences of welfare leavers. In this volume, we have drawn on information from many location-based studies of leavers and coupled it with national data on families leaving welfare. Our comprehensive synthesis of this research suggests that, by and large, families that left welfare have joined the ranks of the working poor—while they are generally better off than they were on welfare, they still face substantial hardships. Nevertheless, these welfare leavers are the success story of welfare reform. In study after study, we also find that a significant minority of leavers, about one in five, leave welfare without a job, remain jobless for long periods, and have no visible means of support. Understanding how leavers have fared is an important first step in determining if federal or state policy interventions are warranted to help leavers meet their basic needs in the short term and attain self-sufficiency in the long run.

WHAT DO WE KNOW ABOUT WELFARE LEAVERS?

Across the nation, studies consistently show that three out of five welfare leavers work upon exit. Further, four out of five work at some time during the first year after leaving welfare, although only two out of five work consistently. And, when leavers do work, they usually work full time and earn $7 to $8 an hour—well above the federal minimum wage. Their annual incomes hover around the poverty line and a substantial portion (25 to 50 percent) experience material hardships like food or housing insecurity.

The substantial share of leavers who work is often considered to be a sign of welfare reform's success and rightfully so, but it is not an unqualified success. Families leaving welfare for work are climbing the economic ladder, but their struggles still merit the attention of policymakers. Indeed, working leavers need help to stay at work and make ends meet.

Further, not all leavers exited welfare for work—they are a diverse group. Some nonworking leavers return to welfare quickly; about one in five leavers return within one year of exit. Some leavers choose not to work because they have a working spouse/partner or a friend or other family member who supports them. Also, some have transitioned from welfare to a disability program such as SSI, which usually provides a higher level of assistance than TANF does to those who cannot work. Finally, 10 to 12 percent of families that leave welfare have no earnings and receive no transfer payment—indeed, they have no visible means of support. Some may have left welfare involuntarily due to a sanction or time limit, and they tend to face significant barriers to work and experience substantial material hardship.

WHAT CAN GOVERNMENTS DO TO HELP FAMILIES LEAVE AND STAY OFF WELFARE?

The most important factor in helping families move from welfare to work is the availability of jobs that can be filled by welfare recipients. On average, adult welfare recipients have no education beyond high school and have limited work experience. As such, the jobs for which they qualify have lower skill requirements and commensurately low pay. Nevertheless, without such employment opportunities, families on welfare would be unable to move into the job market. An obvious precursor for employment opportunities for less-skilled workers is a vibrant economy.

In addition, we need to keep making work pay for those who do enter the low-wage labor market. Existing programs and benefits such as Food Stamps, Medicaid, and the EITC all work to bolster the economic status of low-earning workers. The hardships confronting working leavers could be reduced if more availed themselves of these supports. Increasing take-up of these programs through increasing awareness and making access easier is important. Some states have conducted outreach campaigns and simplified application and recertification procedures for Food Stamps and Medicaid to this end, and there are some early indications that participation is improving (Loprest 2003). Improving access should improve take-up and will likely reduce the material hardships working leavers experience.

Many working leavers never apply for transitional Medicaid coverage even though they are not offered or cannot afford employer-sponsored health insurance. Extending Medicaid coverage as a matter of course for three months after a TANF exit would give former recipients time to apply for and enroll in transitional Medicaid. A lack of health insurance reduces the amount and quality of health care one receives and can lead working leavers to return to the welfare rolls. And as we saw in Chapter 5, many leavers report they are not working for health reasons. Consequently, it is important that families take advantage of the public insurance options available to them.

Moving from welfare to work is easier if people are much better off working than on welfare. To encourage welfare recipients to start working, many states disregard a substantial portion of earnings when determining benefits, at least for the first few months of working. One problem with this method is that when a family combines welfare and work, their lifetime limit clock keeps ticking. States and the federal government should consider "stop the clock" policies that do not count months in which a family works and receives welfare against their lifetime limit.

Finally, the tax code provides one of the biggest rewards of working for low-income families with children: the EITC. Indeed, a single mother of two children earning between $10,350 and $13,550 a year qualifies for the entire credit of $4,140 in 2002. This effectively increases the family income by 30 to 40 percent. States can reinforce the work incentive effects of the federal EITC by providing state EITCs.

Even when the economy is on solid footing, there may be a dearth of entry-level jobs. Consequently, government can encourage private sector employers to create entry-level jobs through a program of targeted subsidies. For example, employers in high unemployment areas who increase the number of workers they employ could receive subsidies for a limited time. While the evidence on the efficacy of past targeted-subsidy efforts has been mixed, this policy option cannot be overlooked (Bartik 2001).

Other ways to improve the material well-being of working leavers are increasing the minimum wage or implementing "living wage" programs. A modest increase in the minimum wage is likely to have limited effectiveness for this population, since most working leavers already earn more than the minimum wage. Elevating the minimum wage by 60 or 70 percent is likely to have nontrivial disemployment effects. Living wage programs usually apply to medium and large firms that do business with local governments, although some cities have passed broader coverage. As a condition of receiving government contracts, employers are required to pay their employees a living wage, which is usually much higher than the minimum wage. Evidence shows that living wages have led to increases in the earnings of low-wage workers generally but also to loss of low-wage jobs in these areas. On net, these policies can lead to decreases in poverty (Adams and Neumark 2003).

A final important benefit for working families is the availability of adequate, affordable child care. Although some working leavers have school-age children or have friends or relatives who will watch their children while they are at work, some leavers need to use paid child care providers; without child care, they simply cannot work. Consequently, it is important to ensure that both adequate funding is available to help working leavers and other low-income workers pay for child care and that there are an adequate number of child care providers to meet the demand. So far, although child care funds increased substantially with welfare reform, evidence is unclear on whether current funding meets the need.

In addition to these income and benefit supports, former welfare recipients can benefit from other service supports as well. For example, some welfare offices have programs to provide post-employment supports and retention services for former recipients. These programs can include job mentors at the workplace, to help navigate the ins and outs of a new job, and provision of emergency assistance, such as funds for car repair. Provision of this assistance can forestall job loss and returns to welfare. Other programs focus on advancement for those in low-wage entry-level jobs. While little is known about which services are most effective, the Administration for Children and Families of the USDHHS is sponsoring an ongoing evaluation of a number of these programs, called the Employment Retention and Advancement evaluation (Anderson and Martinson 2003).

Even with post-employment services, however, some working leavers will lose their jobs. Rather than returning to welfare while seeking employment and burning up months against their lifetime limit, it may be appropriate to steer unemployed leavers into the UI system. Because of earnings and hours requirements, many working leavers will not qualify for UI benefits when they lose their jobs. By granting special status to working welfare leavers within state UI systems, leavers can receive short-term financial assistance while they look for new jobs without having to return to welfare.

WHAT'S NEXT?

The 1996 PRWORA was a titanic change in U.S. welfare policy. Its effects cannot be determined by examining only the first five years of implementation. The true long-run outcomes for recipients, former recipients, and potential recipients will be played out over a much longer time span. In fact, two important factors that are not reflected in the outcomes researched to date need to be considered: the effects of a declining economy and the impact of five-year limits on benefits.

The booming economy and low unemployment rates of the mid to late 1990s certainly influenced the success of welfare-to-work policies and the impact of welfare changes on the lives of recipients. Since economic growth has stalled and unemployment rates began rising in 2001, the challenge of moving families from welfare to work is more daunting. The economic downturn undoubtedly will make it more difficult for recipients to find jobs and could delay some families' exits from welfare. Welfare caseloads during fiscal year 2002 increased for half of states. When caseloads increase, direct payments to recipients increase, leaving less block grant money for services and innovative work programs, particularly those that serve the hard to employ. Because many states are struggling with large budget deficits, state-funded services for recipients are open to cuts (Finegold et al. 2003).

In addition, the results reported in this book by and large do not include the effects of the federal five-year limit on benefits. In many states, families first hit this benefit limit in 2002. How this will impact the composition and economic well-being of welfare leavers remains to be seen. In the past many families left welfare before five years, but many returned, continuing to use up their limited benefits. The true effects on families of having no more lifetime eligibility remain to be seen.

We would not be researchers if we did not end with a plea for more research. The fact is, passage of these reforms spawned a great deal of new research. But just when more research is necessary—to measure longer term outcomes, assess total post-implementation impacts, and to inform potential future policy changes—interest and funding wane. One of the impressive aspects of the research generated after the passage of reforms is that many states increased their capacity to measure outcomes of interest to their state. It is important that these activities continue and are built on, especially in this new era of state flexibility to tailor welfare programs. But, as revenues dip and states scrutinize where to make budget cuts, these activities are in jeopardy. This state-level problem suggests a continuing role for the federal government in funding this kind of capacity building at the state level. The USDHHS has played a key role in this development since 1996 and continues to do so through current funding of local studies on welfare recipients.

In addition, broader efforts to continue research on how leavers are faring should be undertaken. While much basic information can be garnered from linked administrative data, survey data can provide a much fuller picture of the status of welfare leavers. Syntheses of individual place-based surveys of welfare leavers, like this volume, are useful, but because of issues of cross-site comparability, they provide, at best, a patchwork understanding of how welfare leavers are doing. Similarly, national studies using current data are limited because general-use data sets do not have a sufficiently large number of families leaving welfare at the same time to allow for comprehensive analyses. Consequently, it would be useful to have a national survey of welfare leavers with samples drawn from state administrative data. Detailed uniform data on a national sample of leavers—especially if those data are longitudinal, capturing leavers at, for example, 6, 18, and 36 months after exit—would be an important resource for research. Such data would provide a comprehensive picture of welfare leavers across the nation and allow researchers to examine how local policies, practices, and circumstances affect the status of these families.

Some view social welfare policy of the 1990s as a grand social experiment. Although leaver studies are not an evaluation of this experiment, they do provide valuable information on the outcomes of families affected by this policy change. The leaver studies show that if the ultimate goal of welfare policy is to create a system that provides temporary assistance to families on their way to self-sufficiency, we are moving forward but have a long way to go.

Appendix A
Issues in Comparing and Synthesizing Leaver Studies

Even though the leaver studies considered here all take the same basic approach to assessing the status of families leaving welfare, there are important differences across these studies that should be kept in mind when comparing them and drawing general conclusions from them. These differences fall into two broad categories: 1) differences in precisely how the studies were conducted, and 2) differences between the study sites. Because there are so many factors contributing to the well-being of leavers, it is difficult to ascribe differences in outcomes across studies to any specific difference in methods or context. In addition, all of these differences cannot be taken into account simultaneously. However, these differences should be noted as they come to bear on comparisons across studies.

DIFFERENCES IN SPECIFIC METHODS USED AND STUDY IMPLEMENTATION

Leaver studies do not all focus on the same time period. Indeed, some studies focus on leavers from late 1998 while others examine leavers from late 1996 and early 1997. The survey components of the leaver studies also cover different periods of time after leaving. For example, one leaver study interviews leavers more than two years after exit from welfare, while others conduct interviews six months after exit.

Further, although the survey instruments generally gather similar information, a separate team of researchers developed each survey. Each survey focuses on topics of interest in a particular state or locality, leading to differences in measured outcomes. In addition, how well survey respondents represent the population of welfare leavers affects the reliability of survey findings.

Finally, there are some small variations in how the studies define leavers and the types of leavers studied. For example, most but not all studies require a family to remain off welfare for two months to be considered a leaver. Further, some studies focus exclusively on single-parent welfare leavers while others include information on two-parent and, in a few studies, child-only cases. When possible, we present results for single-parent leavers. Some studies, however, present only findings for all leavers, combining single-parent and two-parent cases. The studies that present only combined data are the District of Columbia, Missouri, South Carolina, and Wisconsin. In each case, two-parent leavers represent a relatively small share of the leaver population. Summaries of the types of data used, the time periods analyzed, the study populations, and technical details of surveys appear in Tables A.1 and A.2.

DIFFERENCES BETWEEN STUDY SITES

The economic opportunities prevailing in the states, the welfare policies states have adopted, and the characteristics of welfare recipients themselves likely affect the status of welfare leavers. The impact of economic differences is self-evident. Leavers in states with low unemployment and high wages and incomes are likely to fare better than leavers in states with less favorable economic conditions. The impacts of state TANF policy choices and the characteristics of leavers themselves are less straightforward.

Under TANF block grants, states have substantial flexibility in determining the length of time families can receive cash assistance (time limits), the penalties for not complying with program rules (sanctions), the generosity of cash grants, and how benefits lessen as a family moves from welfare to work. Differences in state policy choices may well affect the rate at which families leave TANF, their employment status and material well-being, and their use of government aid after leaving TANF.

First, consider time limits. Families subject to shorter time limits may feel pressure to leave welfare sooner than families that are years away from exhausting their benefits. Also, leavers who have nearly exhausted their benefits may be more reluctant to return. Next, consider states' sanction policies. In general, states have imposed tiered sanctions, beginning with less severe sanctions and escalating penalties for repeated instances of noncompliance. Note that leavers who were sanctioned off the rolls may be less "job-ready" than other leavers. Further, they may return to TANF at higher rates than nonsanctioned leavers when eligible.

The generosity of a state's welfare program also affects its leavers' outcomes. For example, recipients in states with higher basic benefits and higher earnings disregards can remain on the rolls while working longer than families in less generous states. As a result, leavers in more generous states may have higher incomes than leavers from less generous states in the months following their TANF exits simply because those with lower incomes do not leave the rolls. On the other hand, leavers may be more likely to return to welfare if the program offers generous assistance. Finally, other aspects of states' TANF policies (for example, work requirements and diversion policies) also likely affect the composition of the states' welfare leaver populations.

It is also important to note that states may pursue a mix of policies that are likely to have offsetting effects on the outcomes of leavers—for example, some states may have strict time limits and full family sanctions but generous earnings disregards.

In addition to differences in the economic and policy contexts, differences in the personal characteristics of welfare recipients and welfare leavers must be considered when comparing findings across leaver studies. Indeed, part of any difference in outcomes across sites may be due to differences among leavers themselves. Further, states likely structure their welfare policies with their welfare populations in mind—for example, a state with a high proportion of high school dropouts may emphasize work readiness programs—and this too may affect the status of leavers.

A priori, it is difficult to anticipate whether younger leavers will, on average, fare better or worse than older leavers. While younger leavers probably have fewer children and shorter spells of receipt prior to exit than older leavers, they also probably have younger children and less work experience. It is also difficult to anticipate how racial and ethnic differences may affect leavers' outcomes, because race is only one of many differences among the study areas. Differences in marital status, number of children, and education all have a stronger theoretical link than race or age to the outcomes of welfare leavers. For example, married or previously married leavers may have greater access to

Table A.1 Methodology of Leaver Studies

State	Type of study	Leaver cohort	Definition of leaver	Cases excluded	Key reported subjects
Arizona	Survey and administrative	1Q98	One month, two months	Two-parent units, child-only cases, cases under tribal jurisdiction	Sanctioned, unsanctioned leavers
District of Columbia	Survey and administrative	Two cohorts: 4Q97, 4Q98	One month	Child-only cases	Continuous leavers
Florida	Survey and administrative	2Q97	Two months	Two-parent units, child-only cases	Continuous leavers
Georgia (Bross 2001)	Administrative	Three cohorts: 1Q97, 1Q98, 1Q99	Two months	Two-parent units	Continuous leavers
Georgia (Foster and Rickman 2001)	Survey	Jan. 1999–June 2000	Two months	Two-parent units	Continuous leavers
Illinois	Survey and administrative	Six cohorts: 3Q97, 4Q97, 1Q98, 2Q98, 3Q98, 4Q98; Survey: Dec. 1998	Two months	Child-only cases	Single parents, two parents; Cook County, Downstate
Iowa	Survey and administrative	2Q99	Two months	Two-parent units, child-only cases	Continuous leavers
Massachusetts	Survey and administrative	Dec. 1998– March 1999	Two months	Cases that left the state, child-only cases	Time-limit closing, non–time limit closing
Missouri	Administrative	4Q96	Two months	Child-only cases	n/a
Missouri	Survey	4Q96	Two months	Child-only cases	Kansas City, St. Louis
New York	Administrative	1Q97	Two months	Child-only cases, cases without a social security number, cases closed due to moving out of state, adults without children	Single parents, two parents

South Carolina	Survey and administrative	Oct. 1998–March 1999	Two months	Child-only cases, permanently or temporarily disabled TANF recipients, those with other exemption from work requirements	Continuous leavers; case closure due to earnings, time limits, sanctions; high vs. low risk neighborhood
Washington (Ahn et al. 2000)	Administrative	Three cohorts: 4Q96, 4Q97, 4Q98	Two months	Child-only cases	TANF returners; continuous leavers; single parents, two parents
Washington (Du et al. 2000)	Survey	October 1998	Two months	Child-only cases, two-parent units	TANF returners
Wisconsin	Administrative	2Q98–4Q98	Two months	Child-only cases	Sincle parents, TANF returners; continuous leavers
Cuyahoga County	Survey and administrative	Two cohorts; 3Q96 and 3Q98	Two months	Child-only cases, two-parent units	n/a
Los Angeles County	Administrative	3Q96	Two months	Child-only cases, two-parent units	n/a
Bay Area	Survey and administrative	Two cohorts: 4Q96, 4Q98	Two months	Child-only cases	Single parents, two parents; informally diverted, housing assistance

NOTE: n/a = not available.
SOURCE: See Table A.3 for complete list of leaver studies.

Table A.2 Administrative Data

Study	Topics reported in study	Period of follow-up after exit
Arizona	Employment, TANF, Food Stamps, Medicaid, child care subsidy, child support, child welfare[a]	One year
District of Columbia	Employment, TANF, Food Stamps, Medicaid	18 months
Florida	Employment, TANF, Food Stamps, Medicaid	21 months
Georgia	Employment, TANF, Food Stamps, Medicaid, child support	One year
Illinois	Employment, TANF, Food Stamps, Medicaid, WIC, child care subsidy, Family Case Management Services, Drug and Alcohol Treatment Services, EITC, child support, child welfare[b]	One year
Iowa	Employment, TANF, Food Stamps, Medicaid	One year
Massachusetts	Employment, TANF, Food Stamps	11 months
Missouri	Employment, TANF, Food Stamps, Medicaid	Two years
New York	Employment, TANF, Food Stamps, Medicaid	One year
South Carolina	Employment, TANF, Food Stamps, Medicaid	One year
Washington	Employment, TANF, Food Stamps, Medicaid, child care subsidy, child support programs, child welfare[b]	Two years
Wisconsin	Employment, TANF, Food Stamps, Medicaid	15 months
Cuyahoga County	Employment, TANF, Food Stamps, Medicaid	One year
Los Angeles County	Employment[c]	One year
Bay Area	Employment, TANF, Food Stamps, Medicaid	One year

NOTE: WIC = Women, Infants, and Children Program.

[a] Substantiated child protective service reports, out-of-home placements, and use of emergency services.

[b] Child abuse and neglect referrals and out-of-home placements.

[c] These are the topics covered in preliminary analyses available to the authors at the time these studies were collected. The final report covers additional topics.

SOURCE: See Table A.3 for a complete listing of the leaver studies referenced.

sources of support (for example, child support) than never-married leavers. Leavers with more children may have a harder time balancing work and child rearing than other leavers. Finally, leavers with higher levels of education should have an easier time finding, keeping, and advancing in jobs than less-educated leavers.

It is also important to note that while welfare caseloads declined throughout the United States during the 1990s, the magnitude of the decline varied from state to state. The average leaver from states with large caseload declines may come from "deeper" in the caseload and have more barriers to overcome in moving to work than the average leaver from other states. As such, these leavers may have less success in the labor market, face greater hardships, and be more likely to return to welfare. Note, however, that recent research suggests that leavers are not becoming more disadvantaged over time (Loprest 2001).

Overall, there are some potentially important differences in the characteristics of welfare recipients and leavers across study sites; however, these differences may have offsetting effects on outcomes. For example, one state's leavers may be more educated on average than leavers in other states, but they may tend to have more children.

All these differences between study methods and study sites likely affect leavers' post-TANF experiences. However, it is difficult to derive any simple rules of thumb to aid in comparing findings across studies. The varied policies pursued by the study states likely have offsetting effects on leavers' outcomes. Further, while some states had unambiguously good economies (low unemployment and high incomes), many states had more mixed conditions. And leavers themselves often have a mixed set of characteristics, some more favorable to employment and well-being after exit than others. Thus, it is difficult to ascribe differences in average outcomes across leaver studies to observable differences between study locations. However, understanding these contextual differences may be important when comparing specific outcomes for subgroups of leavers.

Finally, the complete set of leaver studies used in our study is listed in Table A.3.

Table A.3 Leaver Studies Included in this Review

Arizona

Westra, Karen L., and John Routley. 2000. *Arizona Cash Assistance Exit Study: First Quarter 1998 Final Report.* Arizona Department of Economic Security.

District of Columbia

Acs, Gregory, and Pamela Loprest. 2001b. *The Status of TANF Leavers in the District of Columbia: Final Report.* Washington, DC: The Urban Institute.

Florida

Crew, Robert E., Jr., Joe Eyerman, Justin Graham, and Nancy McMillan. 2000. *Tracking the Outcomes of Welfare Reform in Florida for Three Groups of People.* Tallahassee: Florida State University.

Georgia

Bross, N. 2001. *Employment, Earnings, and Recidivism among Georgia's TANF Leavers: Findings from the TANF Follow-up System.* Atlanta: Georgia Department of Human Resources.

Foster, E. Michael, and Dana K. Rickman. 2001. *Life After Welfare: Report of the Georgia Welfare Leavers Study.* Atlanta: Georgia Department of Human Resources, Division of Family and Children Services.Georgia State University.

Illinois

Julnes, George, Anthony Halter, Steven Anderson, Lee Frost-Kumpf, Richard Schuldt, Francis Staskon, and Barbara Ferrara. 2000. *Illinois Study of Former TANF Clients, Final Report.* Institute for Public Affairs, University of Illinois at Springfield, and School of Social Work, University of Illinois at Urbana-Champaign.

Iowa

Kauff, Jacqueline, Lisa Fowler, Thomas Fraker, and Julita Milliner-Waddell. 2001. *Iowa Families That Left TANF: Why Did They Leave And How Are They Faring?* Washington, DC: Mathematica Policy Research.

Massachusetts

Massachusetts Department of Transitional Assistance. 2000. *After Time Limits: A Study of Households Leaving Welfare Between December 1998 and April 1999.* Boston: Massachusetts Department of Transitional Assistance.

Missouri

Midwest Research Institute. 2001. *Economic Outcomes of Former Missouri AFDC Recipients. 1996 Leaver Cohort.* Kansas City, MO: Midwest Research Institute.

Ryan, Sharon. 2001. *Final Report on the 1996 Cohort of Welfare Leavers (Administrative Outcomes).* Columbia MO: University of Missouri.

New York

The Rockefeller Institute of Government, New York State Office of Temporary and Disability Assistance, and the New York State Department of Labor. 1999. *After Welfare: A Study of Work and Benefit Use After Case Closing.* Revised Interim Report. New York: New York State Department of Labor.

South Carolina
Richardson, Phil, Gregg Schoenfeld, Susan LaFever, Frances Jackson, and Mark Tecco. 2001. *Welfare Leavers and Diverters Research Study. One Year Follow-Up of Welfare Leavers—Final Report.* Reston, VA: MAXIMUS, Inc.
Washington
Ahn, Jay, Debra Fogarty, S. Kraley, F. Lai, and L. Deppman. 2000. *A Study of Washington State TANF Departures and Welfare Reform. Welfare Reform and Findings from Administrative Data. Final Report.* Olympia: Washington State Department of Social and Health Services.
Du, J., with D. Fogarty, D. Hopps, and J. Hu. 2000. *A Study of Washington State TANF Leavers and TANF Recipients. Findings from the April–June 1999 Telephone Survey. Final Report.* Olympia WA: Washington State Department of Social and Health Services.
Wisconsin
Wisconsin Department of Workforce Development. 2001. *Wisconsin Works Leavers Survey Final Report: Those Who Left W2 Cash Assistance (April–December 1998.).* Madison, WI: Wisconsin Department of Workforce Development.
Bay Area Study
Mancuso, David C., Charles J. Lieberman, Vanessa L. Lindler, and Anne Moses. 2001. *Examining Circumstances of Individuals and Families Who Leave TANF: Assessing the Validity of Administrative Data.* Burlingame, CA: SPHERE Institute.
Cuyahoga County
Verma, Nandita, Claudia Coulton, R. Hendra, and A. Polousky. 2001. *Monitoring Outcomes for Cuyahoga County's Welfare Leavers: How Are They Faring?* Prepared for Cuyahoga Work and Training. New York: MDRC.
Los Angeles County
Verma, Nandita, and Barbara Goldman. 2000. "Los Angeles County Post-TANF Tracking Project: Quarterly Progress Report." (Preliminary data.) New York: Manpower Demonstration Research Corporation.

NOTE: Many of these reports can be accessed at http://aspe.hhs.gov/hsp/leavers99/reports.htm.

References

Acs, Gregory, and Pamela Loprest. 2001a. *Final Synthesis Report of the Findings from ASPE's Leavers Grants.* Report to the U.S. Department of Health and Human Services. Washington, DC.

———. 2001b. *The Status of TANF Leavers in the District of Columbia: Final Report.* Washington, DC: The Urban Institute.

———. 2002. "Studies of Welfare Leavers: Data, Methods, and Contributions to the Policy Process." In *Studies of Welfare Populations: Data Collection and Research Issues,* Michele Ver Ploeg, Robert A. Moffitt, and Constance F. Citro, eds. Washington, DC: National Academies Press, pp. 385–414.

Acs, Gregory, Katherin Ross Phillips, Caroline Ratcliffe, and Douglas Wissoker. 2001. *Comings and Goings: The Changing Dynamics of Welfare in the 1990s.* Report to the U.S. Department of Health and Human Services. Washington, DC.

Adams, Gina, and Kathleen Snyder. 2003. "Essential but Often Ignored: Child Care Providers in the Subsidy System." *Assessing the New Federalism* Policy Brief A-57. Washington, DC: The Urban Institute.

Adams, Gina, Kathleen Snyder, and Jodi R. Sandfort. 2002. "Getting and Retaining Child Care Assistance: How Policy and Practice Influence Parents' Experiences." *Assessing the New Federalism* occasional paper no. 55. Washington, DC: The Urban Institute.

Adams, Scott, and David Neumark. 2003. "Living Wage Effects: New and Improved Evidence." NBER working paper no. 9702. Cambridge, MA: National Bureau of Economic Research.

Ahn, Jay, Debra Fogarty, S. Kraley, F. Lai, and L. Deppman. 2000. *A Study of Washington State TANF Departures and Welfare Reform. Welfare Reform and Findings from Administrative Data. Final Report.* Olympia, WA: Washington State Department of Social and Health Services.

Anderson, Jacquelyn, and Karin Martinson. 2003. *Service Delivery and Institutional Linkages: Early Implementation Experiences of Employment Retention and Advancement Programs.* New York: MDRC.

Bartik, Timothy J. 2001. *Jobs for the Poor: Can Labor Demand Policies Help?* Washington, DC: The Urban Institute.

Bavier, Richard. 2001. "Welfare Reform Data from the Survey of Income and Program Participation." *Monthly Labor Review* 124(7):13–24.

———. 2002. "Welfare Reform Impacts in the SIPP." *Monthly Labor Review* 125(11): 23–38.

Blank, Rebecca, and Ron Haskins. 2001. *The New World of Welfare.* Washington, DC: Brookings Institution Press.

Brauner, Sarah, and Pamela Loprest. 1999. "Where Are They Now? What States' Studies of People Who Left Welfare Tell Us." *Assessing the New Federalism* Policy Brief A-32. Washington, DC: The Urban Institute.

Bross, N. 2001. *Employment, Earnings, and Recidivism among Georgia's TANF Leavers: Findings from the TANF Follow-up System.* Atlanta: Georgia Department of Human Resources.

Cantor, David, and Patricia Cunningham. 2002. "Methods for Obtaining High Response Rates in Telephone Surveys." In *Studies of Welfare Populations: Data Collection and Research Issues,* Michele Ver Ploeg, Robert A. Moffitt, and Constance F. Citro, eds. Washington, DC: National Academies Press, pp. 55–85.

Cherlin, Andrew, Linda Burton, Judith Francis, Jane Henrici, Laura Lein, James Quane, and Karen Bogen. 2001. "Sanctions and Case Closings for Noncompliance: Who Is Affected and Why." Welfare, Children, and Families Policy Brief 01–1. Baltimore, MD: Johns Hopkins University.

Crew, Robert E., Jr., Joe Eyerman, Justin Graham, and Nancy McMillan. 2000. *Tracking the Outcomes of Welfare Reform in Florida for Three Groups of People.* Tallahassee, FL: Florida State University.

Dalaker, Joseph. 2001. U.S. Census Bureau Current Population Reports, Series P60–214, "Poverty in the United States: 2000." Washington, DC: U.S. Government Printing Office.

Danziger, Sandra, Mary Corcoran, Sheldon Danziger, Colleen Heflin, Ariel Kalil, Judith Levine, Daniel Rosen, Kristin Seefeldt, Kristine Siefert, and Richard Tolman. 2000. "Barriers to the Employment of Welfare Recipients." In *Prosperity for All,* Robert Cherry and William M. Rodgers III, eds. New York: Russell Sage Foundation, pp. 245–277.

Danziger, Sheldon, Colleen M. Heflin, Mary E. Corcoran, Elizabeth Oltmans, and Hui-Chen Wang. 2002. "Does It Pay to Move from Welfare to Work?" *Journal of Policy Analysis and Management* 21(4): 671–692.

Du, J., with D. Fogarty, D. Hopps, and J. Hu. 2000. *A Study of Washington State TANF Leavers and TANF Recipients. Findings from the April–June 1999 Telephone Survey. Final Report.* Olympia, WA: Washington State Department of Social and Health Services.

Dunton, Nancy. 1999. "Non-Response Analysis: Missouri Leavers Survey." Unpublished tables and presentation at the Fall 1999 Outcomes Grantee Meeting of the U.S. Department of Health and Human Services Office of the Assistant Secretary for Planning and Evaluation, Washington, DC, October 25–26.

Edelhoch, Marilyn, and Linda Martin. 1999. "Analysis of Response Rates and Non-Response Bias in Surveys." Unpublished tables and presentation at the Fall 1999 Outcomes Grantee Meeting of the U.S. Department of Health and Human Services Office of the Assistant Secretary for Planning and Evaluation, Washington, DC, October 25–26.

Finegold, Kenneth, Stephanie Schardin, Elaine Maag, Rebecca Steinbach, David Merriman, and Alan Weil. 2003. "Social Program Spending and State Fiscal Crises." *Assessing the New Federalism* occasional paper no. 70. Washington, DC: The Urban Institute.

Foster, E. Michael, and Dana K. Rickman. 2001. *Life After Welfare: Report of the Georgia Welfare Leavers Study.* Atlanta: Georgia Department of Human Resources, Division of Family and Children Services. Georgia State University.

Giannarelli, Linda, Sarah Adelman, and Stefanie Schmidt. 2003. "Getting Help with Child Care Expenses." *Assessing the New Federalism* occasional paper no. 62. Washington, DC: The Urban Institute.

Goerge, Robert, and Bong Joo Lee. 2002. "Matching and Cleaning Administrative Data." In *Studies of Welfare Populations: Data Collection and Research Issues,* Michele Ver Ploeg, Robert A. Moffitt, and Constance F. Citro, eds. Washington, DC: National Academies Press, pp. 197–219.

Greenberg, Mark, and Steve Savner. 1996. *A Detailed Summary of Key Provisions of the Temporary Assistance for Needy Families Block Grant of H.R. 3734.* Washington, DC: Center for Law and Social Policy.

Groves, Robert, and Douglas Wissoker. 1999. "No. 7: Early Nonresponse Studies of the 1997 National Survey of America's Families." National Survey of America's Families Methodology working paper. Washington, DC: The Urban Institute.

Gueron, Judith M., and Gayle Hamilton. 2002. "The Role of Education and Training in Welfare Reform." *Welfare Reform and Beyond* Policy Brief no. 20. Washington, DC: The Brookings Institution.

Hofferth, Sandra, Stephen Stanhope, and Kathleen Harris. 2001. "Exiting Welfare in the 1990s: Did Public Policy Influence Recipients' Behavior?" Photocopy. Department of Family Studies, University of Maryland, College Park, MD.

Hotz, V. Joseph, and John Karl Scholz. 2002. "Measuring Employment and Income for Low-Income Populations with Administrative and Survey Data." In *Studies of Welfare Populations: Data Collection and Research Issues,* Michele Ver Ploeg, Robert A. Moffitt, and Constance F. Citro, eds. Washington, DC: National Academies Press, pp. 275–315.

Johnson, Rucker C., and Mary E. Corcoran. 2003. "The Road to Economic Self-Sufficiency: Job Quality and Job Transition Patterns after Welfare Reform." *Journal of Policy Analysis and Management* 22(4): 615–639.

Julnes, George, Anthony Halter, Steven Anderson, Lee Frost-Kumpf, Richard Schuldt, Francis Staskon, and Barbara Ferrara. 2000. *Illinois Study of For-*

mer TANF Clients, Final Report. Institute for Public Affairs, University of Illinois at Springfield, and School of Social Work, University of Illinois at Urbana-Champaign.

Kauff, Jacqueline, Lisa Fowler, Thomas Fraker, and Julita Milliner-Waddell. 2001. *Iowa Families That Left TANF: Why Did They Leave And How Are They Faring?* Washington, DC: Mathematica Policy Research.

Lee, Bong Joo, Dan A. Lewis, and Amy Bush Stevens. 2001. "The Importance of Transitional Benefits: Who Loses Medicaid and Food Stamps, and What Does It Mean for Staying Off Welfare?" *Illinois Families Study* Policy Brief no. 1. Evanston, IL: Northwestern University, Institute for Policy Research.

Loeb, Susanna, and Mary Corcoran. 2001. "Welfare, Work Experience, and Economic Self-Sufficiency." *Journal of Policy Analysis and Management* 20(1): 1–20.

Loprest, Pamela J. 1999. "Families Who Left Welfare: Who Are They and How Are They Doing?" *Assessing the New Federalism* discussion paper 99–02. Washington, DC: The Urban Institute.

———. 2001. "How Are Families Who Left Welfare Doing Over Time? A Comparison of Two Cohorts of Welfare Leavers." *FRBNY Economic Policy Review.* New York: Federal Reserve Bank of New York.

———. 2002a. "Making the Transition from Welfare to Work: Successes but Continuing Concerns." In *Welfare Reform: The Next Act,* Alan Weil and Kenneth Finegold, eds. Washington, DC: Urban Institute Press, pp. 17–32.

———. 2002b. "Who Returns to Welfare?" *New Federalism: National Survey of America's Families* Brief B-49. Washington, DC: The Urban Institute.

———. 2003. "Use of Government Benefits Increases among Families Leaving Welfare." *Snapshots of America's Families III* No. 6. Washington, DC: The Urban Institute.

Mancuso, David C., Charles J. Lieberman, Vanessa L. Lindler, and Anne Moses. 2001. *Examining Circumstances of Individuals and Families Who Leave TANF: Assessing the Validity of Administrative Data.* Burlingame, CA: SPHERE Institute.

Massachusetts Department of Transitional Assistance. 2000. *After Time Limits: A Study of Households Leaving Welfare Between December 1998 and April 1999.* Boston: Massachusetts Department of Transitional Assistance.

Mathiowetz, Nancy A., Charlie Brown, and John Bound. 2002. "Measurement Error in Surveys of the Low Income Population." In *Studies of Welfare Populations: Data Collection and Research Issues,* Michele Ver Ploeg, Robert A. Moffitt, and Constance F. Citro, eds. Washington, DC: National Academies Press, pp. 157–194.

Midwest Research Institute. 2001. *Economic Outcomes of Former Missouri AFDC Recipients. 1996 Leaver Cohort.* Kansas City, MO: Midwest Research Institute.

Nathan, Richard P., and Thomas L. Gais. 1999. *Implementing the Personal Responsibility Act of 1996: A First Look.* Albany, NY: Rockefeller Institute Press.

Pavetti, LaDonna. 1993. "The Dynamics of Welfare and Work: Exploring the Process by Which Women Work Their Way Off Welfare." Unpublished doctoral dissertation (D-93-1). Cambridge, MA: Harvard University.

Pavetti, LaDonna, Michelle Derr, and Heather Hesketh. 2003. *Review of Sanction Policies and Research Studies: Final Literature Review.* Washington, DC: Mathematica Policy Research.

Rangarajan, Anu, and Robert G. Wood. 2000. *Current and Former WFNJ Clients: How Are They Faring 30 Months Later?* Report to the State of New Jersey, Department of Human Services, Office of Policy and Planning. Princeton, NJ: Mathematica Policy Research.

Richardson, Phil, Gregg Schoenfeld, Susan LaFever, Frances Jackson, and Mark Tecco. 2001. *Welfare Leavers and Diverters Research Study. One Year Follow-Up of Welfare Leavers—Final Report.* Reston, VA: MAXIMUS, Inc.

Richer, Elise, Steve Savner, and Mark Greenberg. 2001. *Frequently Asked Questions About Working Welfare Leavers.* Washington, DC: Center for Law and Social Policy.

The Rockefeller Institute of Government, New York State Office of Temporary and Disability Assistance, and the New York State Department of Labor. 1999. *After Welfare: A Study of Work and Benefit Use After Case Closing.* Revised Interim Report. New York: New York State Department of Labor.

Ryan, Sharon. 2001. *Final Report on the 1996 Cohort of Welfare Leavers (Administrative Outcomes).* Columbia MO: University of Missouri.

Singer, Eleanor, and Richard A. Kulka. 2002. "Paying Respondents for Survey Participation." In *Studies of Welfare Populations: Data Collection and Research Issues,* Michele Ver Ploeg, Robert A. Moffitt, and Constance F. Citro, eds. Washington, DC: National Academies Press, pp. 105–128.

U.S. Department of Agriculture. 1999. *Household Food Security in the United States 1995–1998* (Advance Report). Washington, DC: USDA Food and Nutrition Service.

———. 2003. *Food Stamp Program State Options Report.* Washington, DC: USDA Food and Nutrition Service.

U.S. Department of Health and Human Services. 2000. "TANF 'Leavers,' Applicants, and Caseload Studies: Summary of Research on Welfare Outcomes Funded by ASPE." Washington, DC: U.S. Department of Health and Human Services, Office of the Assistant Secretary for Planning and Evaluation. Available at http://aspe.hhs.gov/hsp/leavers99/ombsum.htm (accessed in March 2004).

U.S. General Accounting Office (USGAO). 1999. *Welfare Reform: Information on Former Recipients' Status.* GAO-HEHS-99–48. Washington, DC: U.S. General Accounting Office.

———. 2000. *Welfare Reform: State Sanction Policies and Number of Families Affected.* GAO-HEHS-00–44. Washington, DC: U.S. General Accounting Office.

Verma, Nandita, Claudia Coulton, R. Hendra, and A. Polousky. 2001. *Monitoring Outcomes for Cuyahoga County's Welfare Leavers: How Are They Faring?* Prepared for Cuyahoga Work and Training. New York: MDRC.

Verma, Nandita, and Barbara Goldman. 2000. "Los Angeles County Post-TANF Tracking Project: Quarterly Progress Report." (Preliminary data.) New York: Manpower Demonstration Research Corporation.

Weiss, Charlene, and Barbara A. Bailar. 2002. "High Response Rates for Low Income Population in In-Person Surveys." In *Studies of Welfare Populations: Data Collection and Research Issues,* Michele Ver Ploeg, Robert A. Moffitt, and Constance F. Citro, eds. Washington, DC: National Academies Press, pp. 86–104.

Westra, Karen L., and John Routley. 2000. *Arizona Cash Assistance Exit Study: First Quarter 1998 Final Report.* Arizona Department of Economic Security.

Wisconsin Department of Workforce Development. 2001. *Wisconsin Works Leavers Survey Final Report: Those Who Left W2 Cash Assistance (April–December 1998).* Madison, WI: Wisconsin Department of Workforce Development.

Wood, Robert G., and Anu Rangarajan. 2003. "What's Happening to TANF Leavers Who Are Not Employed?" *Issue Brief* no. 6. Washington, DC: Mathematica Policy Research.

Zedlewski, Sheila. 2001. "Former Welfare Families and the Food Stamp Program: The Exodus Continues." *Assessing the New Federalism* Brief B-33. Washington, DC: The Urban Institute.

———. 2002. "Family Incomes: Rising, Falling, or Holding Steady?" In *Welfare Reform: The Next Act,* Alan Weil and Kenneth Finegold, eds. Washington, DC: Urban Institute Press, pp. 53–78.

The Authors

Gregory Acs is a senior research associate in The Urban Institute's Income and Benefits Policy Center. He holds a Ph.D. in economics and social work from the University of Michigan. Dr. Acs's research focuses on welfare policy and the well-being of low-income families and children. In addition to his work on current and former welfare recipients, Dr. Acs has examined how 1996's welfare reforms have affected children's living arrangements as well as the implications of recent trends in living arrangements on the well-being of children. He has also examined how state policy choices and federal laws affect the incentives families face as they move from welfare to work.

Pamela Loprest is a labor economist and senior research associate at the Urban Institute. She received her Ph.D. in economics from the Massachusetts Institute of Technology. Dr. Loprest's research focuses on low-wage labor markets and barriers to work among disadvantaged populations. In addition to her work on former welfare recipients, she has studied barriers to work among welfare recipients and the impact on work behavior and how to structure programs to support work among persons with disabilities.

Index

The italic letters *f*, *n*, and *t* following a page number indicate that the subject information of the heading is within a figure, note, or table, respectively, on that page.

About the Institute

The W.E. Upjohn Institute for Employment Research is a nonprofit research organization devoted to finding and promoting solutions to employment-related problems at the national, state, and local levels. It is an activity of the W.E. Upjohn Unemployment Trustee Corporation, which was established in 1932 to administer a fund set aside by the late Dr. W.E. Upjohn, founder of The Upjohn Company, to seek ways to counteract the loss of employment income during economic downturns.

The Institute is funded largely by income from the W.E. Upjohn Unemployment Trust, supplemented by outside grants, contracts, and sales of publications. Activities of the Institute comprise the following elements: 1) a research program conducted by a resident staff of professional social scientists; 2) a competitive grant program, which expands and complements the internal research program by providing financial support to researchers outside the Institute; 3) a publications program, which provides the major vehicle for disseminating the research of staff and grantees, as well as other selected works in the field; and 4) an Employment Management Services division, which manages most of the publicly funded employment and training programs in the local area.

The broad objectives of the Institute's research, grant, and publication programs are to 1) promote scholarship and experimentation on issues of public and private employment and unemployment policy, and 2) make knowledge and scholarship relevant and useful to policymakers in their pursuit of solutions to employment and unemployment problems.

Current areas of concentration for these programs include causes, consequences, and measures to alleviate unemployment; social insurance and income maintenance programs; compensation; workforce quality; work arrangements; family labor issues; labor-management relations; and regional economic development and local labor markets.